For Art Ring,

Peter Miesen

JOHN
STEINBECK

Nature and Myth

JOHN STEINBECK
Nature and Myth

PETER LISCA

THOMAS Y. CROWELL COMPANY   NEW YORK

Portions of this book have previously appeared
in different form as follows: a discussion of "The Raid"
in *Steinbeck Quarterly* (Summer–Fall), 1972; the influence
of the *Tao Te Ching* on *Cannery Row* in *San Jose Studies*,
November 1975; the chapter on *Cup of Gold* and *To a God Unknown*
in *Kwartalnik Neofilologiczny* (Warsaw), Vol. XXII, 1975.

Library of Congress Cataloging in Publication Data
Lisca, Peter.
John Steinbeck, nature and myth.
(Twentieth-century American writers)
Bibliography: p.
Includes index.
SUMMARY: Portrays the life and achievements
of a distinguished American writer, winner of a Nobel prize
in 1962 and author of "Grapes of Wrath" and "Travels with Charlie."
1. Steinbeck, John, 1902-1968. 2. Novelists, American—
20th century—Biography. [1. Steinbeck, John, 1902-1968
2. Authors, American] I. Title. PS3537.T3234Z719   813'.5'2
[B] [92] 77-27031 ISBN 0-690-01315-9 ISBN 0-690-03835-6 lib. bdg.

*For Amy
and our children,
Catherine and Colleen*

Acknowledgments

I wish to express my gratitude to those many students and critics of Steinbeck from whom I have learned more than I can here specifically acknowledge.

CONTENTS

JOHN
STEINBECK
Nature and Myth

1

✻✻✻✻✻✻✻

Outward from California:

A LIFE OF CHANGES

JOHN STEINBECK was born in Salinas, California, on February 27, 1902, the same year in which died the two most prominent American writers who had become known as Californians— Bret Harte and Frank Norris. To have been born and raised in California was an important factor in Steinbeck's development, but not because he ever became a regional writer or a local colorist. Unlike his contemporary Southern writers, the environment did not lead him to an obsession with local themes and character types. The small ranch and farm people of *The Long Valley, The Pastures of Heaven,* and *The Red Pony* lack the strong local color found in regional literature.

In Dubious Battle, Of Mice and Men, and much of *The Grapes of Wrath* are concerned with current regional themes and situations, but always Steinbeck mutes the elements of local color and works instead for a universality of reference. His longest novel, *East of Eden,* has much of California in it, as it deals in part with the history of his own family and as the climactic action is set in the present and takes place in Steinbeck's home county. But the subject matter looms larger than the setting. Perhaps of his California novels, *Tortilla Flat* and *Cannery Row* come closest to being regional fiction, and it is interesting that in this respect they are rivaled by his last novel, *The Winter of Our Discontent,* which has a small New England coastal town for its setting.

All this is not to say that Steinbeck's California background is unimportant in a consideration of his work. There is obviously his use of the kinds of people, themes, and natural surroundings that were intimate and well known to him from early childhood. But beyond that, as we shall see in discussing his novels and stories, the variety and vastness of the landscape and the Pacific Ocean, which whispers on the sands of Monterey Bay and breaks against the cliffs of Point Lobos farther south, provided Steinbeck with a symbolism and a unique frame of reference for his understanding of the human condition.

On his father's side, John Steinbeck was descended from a German family of Elberfeld (near Düsseldorf), whose name was Grosssteinbeck. His paternal grandfather, John Adolph, together with an older brother, accompanied their sister and her husband, a Lutheran minister, to Jerusalem. There the two brothers met and married the Dickson sisters, two young women from Massachusetts, and after some hilarious adventures about which Steinbeck would write in later life, John Adolph and his wife came to the United States, settling first in New Jersey and then in Florida. There the writer's father, John Ernst Steinbeck, was born in St. Augustine, and his grandfather, John Adolph, was drafted into the Confederate Army. After his discharge John Adolph lived for several years in Massachusetts and then crossed the country to California, establishing a flour mill in Hollister, about fifteen miles northeast of Salinas.

In 1890 John Ernst, then living in Monterey County, married Olive Hamilton, a schoolteacher. Her father, Samuel Hamilton (a significant figure in *East of Eden*) had left the region of Londonderry, Ireland, to sail around the Horn and establish himself in California in 1851. After moving about for a few years (Paso Robles, King City), John and Olive Steinbeck finally settled in Salinas. There they raised a family of three daughters and one son—their third child, named John Ernst after his father. Salinas was then a quiet agricultural trading center, serving the farms and ranches scattered through the Salinas Valley and adjoining areas. Steinbeck senior was in the flour-milling business and prominent enough to be appointed treasurer of Monterey County in 1924, when the incumbent died, and thereafter was regularly elected to that office until a year before his own death in 1936; his wife Olive had died two years earlier. Thus neither parent lived to see their son's emergence into the front rank of American writers.

In his boyhood the writer attended public school in Salinas. He was a good student, interested in a wide variety of subjects; he wrote pieces for the high school paper, *El Gabilan*, participated in track and basketball, and was elected president of his senior class.

Steinbeck's most important experiences, however, came not from school activities but in his home and out in the countryside. As a young boy he had available to him the books that his mother had collected in her years as a teacher. Among them were works by the popular novelists of the time, such as Zane Grey, James Oliver Curwood, Jack London, and James Branch Cabell. In addition, there were the works of Robert Louis Stevenson, who had lived briefly in nearby Monterey, and George Eliot. As a grown man, Steinbeck remembered that in childhood he had first read *Crime and Punishment, Madame Bovary, Paradise Lost,* and *The Return of the Native.* He also read the Bible, both in Episcopal Sunday school and at home, and it became an important influence on the style and themes of his fiction. Another influence was the cycle of stories about King Arthur which he came to know in Sir Thomas Malory's *Morte d'Arthur,* the first book that was his own, at the age of nine. So taken was he with those tales of knightly chivalry that he and his younger sister would frequently act them out. His interest in the Arthurian cycle led him to the form and language of his fourth novel, *Tortilla Flat,* and persisted to the end of his life, at which time he was engaged in doing a version of the tales in modern English. This unfinished work, *The Acts of King Arthur and His Noble Knights,* was published posthumously in 1976.

The lovely California countryside that surrounds Salinas was easily accessible to the young Steinbeck. With his family he made frequent trips to the Monterey Peninsula—Pacific Grove, Monterey, Carmel (nearly twenty miles to the west) and to the area east of King City (forty miles to the south), where his mother's family had a ranch. During the holidays and vacations of his high school years, he sometimes worked on nearby farms and ranches. The sensitivity to nature in all her moods and forms that is ascribed to the boy Jody in *The Red Pony,* Steinbeck later admitted, was part of his own youth. Twenty years later, in the opening pages of *East of Eden,* he again recalls how it was to grow up in this "long valley" of the Salinas River with the gentle, light Gabilan Mountains to the east, the dark, tragic Santa Lucia Mountains to the west, the streams, grasses, animals, and people. And in *Travels With Charley,* published in 1962, the view of this valley from Fremont's Peak is the climax of the book.

After his graduation from Salinas High School in 1919, Steinbeck went to Stanford University and continued studying there intermittently until June 1925. He never, however, earned a degree. Although he enrolled as a major in English, he later announced he was not a candidate for a degree and gave full rein to his own interests, choosing courses from all over the curriculum, including one in marine biology. Further-more, he could not seem to finish any academic year, but took off so many quarters that he earned only about half the credits required for graduation. During these absences he worked on various ranches, on a labor crew building the first road below Big Sur, and in a sugar-beet factory. He did, however, take writing courses at Stanford, where he came under the influence and encouragement of Edith Ronald Mirrielees, his instructor in short-story writing; and during this period, having already determined to become a writer, he was sending out manu-scripts and receiving rejection slips. The Stanford *Spectator* published one of his short stories and a satiric sketch in 1924.

In November 1925, still determined to make writing his profession despite his parents' wishes that he become a lawyer, he worked his way east on a freighter sailing from San Fran-cisco and arrived in New York City with just three dollars in his pocket. He had to borrow money for a hotel room from his sister's husband, who also got him a job as a laborer in the construction of Madison Square Garden. For a little over a month he worked ten, twelve, sometimes eighteen hours a day, pushing wheelbarrows of concrete and living in a cold-water walk-up apartment in Brooklyn. When that job ended, an uncle who had numerous advertising connections got him a job as a reporter on the New York *American* for twenty-five dollars a week. After trying a variety of assignments, including "hu-man-interest" stories and covering the federal courts, he found newspaper work uncongenial and was eventually fired. For a while, he tried to support himself by writing free-lance articles and stories, but without success. He was urged by an editor at Robert M. McBride and Company to do a book of short stories for them. Thus encouraged, Steinbeck stayed on in New York and submitted a manuscript. Unfortunately the editorship had changed in the meantime, and the new management was not interested; the young writer was so enraged that he made quite a scene in the publisher's office. His money ran out, and eventually, weak from hunger, he went back to manual labor. Fortunately, a friend told him of an opportunity to work his way back to California on a freighter. His first New York sojourn left such scars that fifteen years later, even though he was now welcomed as a celebrity, he claimed that he conducted his business there with the watchful care of a Saint Anthony among temptations, and left the city with the virtuous feeling of one who has escaped the whore of Babylon.

Clinging to his literary ambitions, he took various temporary jobs in San Francisco, Salinas, Monterey, and as caretaker of a lodge on Lake Tahoe, high in the Sierras on the Nevada border. Later he worked in a nearby fish hatchery. It was during the two lonely winters that he spent in the Sierras that he wrote his first novel, *Cup of Gold*, which was published with very little notice in 1929. Despite his dissatisfaction with the novel, however, his letters at this period show him more determined than ever to become a writer. He thought that *Cup of Gold* had purged all his "preciousness" and autobiographical tendencies, and that now he would settle down to write "some very

doing a series of articles. But his agents' counsel to finish his novel, and perhaps the lack of finances, caused him to abandon these schemes; once again he was forced to take employment. That winter he returned to Pacific Grove, continued to work on his novel, and in February 1933 sent off the manuscript of *To a God Unknown*, which was published that fall. Like its predecessors, this third published novel was also a commercial failure. Steinbeck had now been writing professionally for eight years; he had earned, all told, perhaps something less than a thousand dollars, most of it in advances that his publishers never recovered from the sale of his work. It sometimes seemed as if Steinbeck's books had come to the attention only of a committee of irate Pacific Grove citizens who demanded that his work be removed from the shelves of the public library. The only silver lining visible in his career was the publication that same winter of the first two parts of *The Red Pony* in the *North American Review*. These short stories were so well liked that the following year the magazine published two more of them: "The Murder" and "The Raid." The latter was selected as an O. Henry prize story for 1934, and the following March another story by Steinbeck, "The White Quail," appeared in the *North American Review*. While he was still working on *To a God Unknown*, he had started thinking about his next book, which he conceived of writing in short episodes like *The Pastures of Heaven*, the reviews of which he was now reading with great scorn. Steinbeck sent the manuscript of this new book, *Tortilla Flat*, to his agents in December of 1933; it was turned down by perhaps as many as eleven publishers before it was accepted by a new firm, Covici-Friede. Published in May 1935, it was this small, local-color novel that first brought Steinbeck to the attention of a wide audience, the public buying it in sufficient numbers to keep it on the best-seller lists for several months. Ironically, *Tortilla Flat* was at one and the same time denounced by the Monterey Chamber of Commerce—who thought it painted a picture of the area that might discourage tourists—and awarded the California Commonwealth Club's annual gold medal for the best novel by a California writer. It was even purchased by Paramount Pictures for what seemed to its author to be the astronomical sum of four thousand dollars, and Steinbeck was offered a contract to work on the screenplay. But he had been hoping to go to Mexico since 1932. In the autumn, after he had signed a contract for six books with Covici-Friede, he and his wife went there in an old battered car. The manuscript of his next book, *In Dubious Battle*, which Steinbeck had completed three months before the appearance of *Tortilla Flat*, was already in the hands of his new publishers. He had intended to stay a long while in Mexico, during which he would continue to work at the amazing pace which had produced five published novels in as many years plus about half the stories that were to appear in 1938 in the short-story collection *The Long Valley*. He found it difficult, however, to write in Mexico. The Steinbecks returned to Pacific Grove late that same year.

Meanwhile Steinbeck's publishers were having their difficulties with the new novel, *In Dubious Battle*. They were worried that coming so soon after the charming and humorous *Tortilla Flat*, a highly controversial labor novel about a strike would hurt Steinbeck's public image and the book's sales. Its main characters are two Communist organizers who foment a violent but justifiable strike of migrant workers. But Steinbeck would not concern himself with what he considered trifles. He wanted no tag of humorist or of any other kind. When an editor at Covici-Friede pointed out certain deviations from accepted party ideology in the behavior of the book's Communist labor organizers and suggested certain changes, Steinbeck instructed his agents to place the manuscript elsewhere. Nor would he consent to the removal of four-letter words and other expletives used by the workers. Covici-Friede was finally allowed to have the manuscript only on condition they would publish it as it was. They did so with some reluctance, fearing that the Communist affiliations of the protagonists might keep the book from selling. Steinbeck did not care about the sales. He knew he had handled an explosive, controversial topic as objectively yet as powerfully and sympathetically as he could. He had no political ax to grind. His information had come from several active Communist labor organizers and from what he himself had been able to observe as an agricultural worker. And although the main events of the strike had actually occurred a few years earlier near Fresno, California, Steinbeck disguised this by altering the book's location and crop. He was writing a novel, he said, not a tract. As it turned out, he was writing what would prove to be the best strike novel yet published in the United States.

Since returning from Mexico late in 1935, Steinbeck's wife, Carol, had been suffering from a sinus condition constantly aggravated by the coastal fogs of the Monterey Peninsula. In the summer of 1936 they therefore left Pacific Grove for a house they had built in the Santa Cruz Mountains, near Los Gatos, about forty-six miles north and ten miles inland from the coast. Although the producer Herman Shumlin wanted Steinbeck to turn *In Dubious Battle* into a play, Steinbeck refused, partly because he had a reluctance to rework his material once it was finished and partly because he felt that the times were changing so fast that the book was already a piece of the past. Besides, he was at work on a new book, something that probably had been under way since early in 1935, when he had mentioned he was working on a play. The manuscript of this new book, *Of Mice and Men,* did not reach his agents until late August 1936.

Many things had intervened—preoccupation with the publishing problems posed by his strike novel, the trip to Mexico, and the completion of another section of *The Red Pony—* "The Leader of the People." Also, in May 1936 he had been planning a trip with Ed Ricketts to Baja California to collect octopi during the low spring tides. That same month half his manuscript book, representing two full months of work, was completely destroyed by a bored setter puppy who had been left alone in the house one night.

Of Mice and Men was published in January 1937. The first of Steinbeck's books to be eagerly awaited by both critics and the reading public, it was tremendously successful. It was a Book-of-the-Month Club choice; its author was named as one of the Ten Outstanding Young Men of the Year. He was thirty-five years old.

Meanwhile, *In Dubious Battle* had made Steinbeck known as a writer conversant with labor conditions in his native state. After finishing *Of Mice and Men*, he accepted assignments to write a number of articles about "the migrants"—those agricultural workers who travel from job to job with the changing crops and seasons. He visited the area around Salinas and the squatters' camps near Bakersfield, 150 miles to the southeast. "Dubious Battle in California" appeared in the magazine *The Nation* (September 12, 1936), and his series of seven articles called "The Harvest Gypsies" in the *San Francisco News* (October 5–12, 1936). Steinbeck had been aware of the problems of agricultural labor in California since boyhood, but during this period he was doing a good deal of firsthand, close investigation. He had made similar trips in preparation for writing *In Dubious Battle*, and he continued to make them after his articles were finished. His method was not to present himself notebook in hand and interview people. Instead he worked and traveled with the migrants as one of them, living as they did and arousing no suspicion from employers militantly alert against outside "agitators" of any kind. In his articles as in his novels, Steinbeck avoided aligning himself politically. Once he refused a commission to do an article for a periodical because the editor asked for a certain political slant.

Steinbeck's agents now began to have increased success in placing his short stories. Although in 1937 "The Snake" was rejected by the *Atlantic* and *Harper's,* and although "Flight," certainly one of his best, was rejected by *Scribner's* and the *Saturday Evening Post,* "The Chrysanthemums," "The Promise," and "The Ears of Johnny Bear" were published that same year in *Esquire, Harper's,* and the *Atlantic* respectively. These and other stories (fifteen, including all four sections of *The Red Pony*) were published as *The Long Valley* the following year. This change of fortune plus the excellent sales of *Of Mice and Men* provided him with a sense of financial security that made it possible for him to indulge his appetite for travel. In the spring of 1937 he and his wife embarked from San Francisco as passengers on a freighter via the Panama Canal to Philadelphia, where they took a train to New York. They arrived on the night of a commemorative banquet for Thomas Mann, which Steinbeck reluctantly attended in a borrowed dinner jacket, and which he left in the middle of the speeches, finding them embarrassing. He visited with his agents (McIntosh and Otis) and his new publishers (the Viking Press) for whom Pascal Covici was now editor. Steinbeck's shyness and dislike of publicity was such that he consented to being interviewed by the press only after much persuasion and fortification with a bottle of whiskey which he kept beside him during the interview and behind which he was photographed.

At the end of March, Steinbeck and his wife, Carol, sailed for Europe aboard a freighter. They traveled in the Soviet Union, Scandinavia, and Ireland, especially in the area around Londonderry, from which his maternal grandfather had come. They returned to New York some three months later, again traveling by freighter—their favorite mode of transportation— and went to stay with George S. Kaufman on his farm in Bucks County, Pennsylvania, where Steinbeck was able to profit from that playwright's suggestions for putting his novelette *Of Mice and Men* into acting form. It was a particularly fortunate association, as Kaufman was also to direct the play on Broadway, and it received the Drama Critics Circle Award for that season. But Steinbeck did not stay for opening night, leaving New York even prior to rehearsals.

Back in California, Steinbeck soon immersed himself again in the plight of the migrant workers. He was not, however, merely researching materials for his next book, but passionately involved in the suffering and injustice. At one time, in fact, he even considered temporarily abandoning his own writing to take a job in Hollywood revising *Of Mice and Men* for the screen, so that he could use the money to help the migrant workers. He was dissuaded by his editor, Pascal Covici, who flew out to California to reason with him. Again early in the following year (1938), he interrupted his writing in order to do what he could to help the deplorable plight of the migrant families, one group of whom were suffering from disease, including smallpox, without adequate medical attention, twenty of them quarantined in one tent and two of the women expecting babies within a week. He compared the suffering of the children in these valleys with that of children in the Spanish Civil War. His own writing seemed trivial to him in comparison. In March *Life* magazine commissioned him to do a feature article on the migrants, and supplied him with a photographer. Steinbeck accepted only expense money for this work, as it seemed to him immoral that he should profit from such suffering, his fee going to help some of the migrants. (The article did not appear until more than a year later, after the publication of *The Grapes of Wrath.*) No doubt it was the depth of such feelings that he poured into a sixty-thousand-word novel about vigilante brutality upon the migrant workers. Although completed, and announced variously by his agents and publishers as "Oklahoma" and "Lettuceberg," Steinbeck did not send it off because he came to see that it was a work of propaganda, the aim of which was "to cause hatred through partial understanding."

He went back to his writing, and late that year mailed to his agents the completed manuscript of *The Grapes of Wrath.* He had worked so hard on this book, and with so much emotional intensity, that when it was finished he collapsed and was confined to bed for some weeks and forbidden to read or write. His involvement in the whole situation was remarkable in that he did not allow his obvious sympathy for the migrants to compromise the discipline of his art, and he refused to exploit in any way his knowledge and reputation for the purpose of personal aggrandizement. As he had not stayed in New York to bask in the limelight attending the opening of *Of Mice and Men* on Broadway, so now he refused to have bound into the novel a page reproduced in his own handwriting; he also refused to enter into various promotional stunts to increase its sales.

The Grapes of Wrath was published in April 1939, and immediately became a national event. It was banned, burned, praised, and debated in the mass media, the schoolrooms, and from the pulpit. The novel was the runaway best seller (over half a million copies in the first edition) of 1939 and in the history of publishing up to that time, second in sales only to *Gone with the Wind.* Steinbeck was accused of being a Communist advocating revolution, and a congressman from Oklahoma, Lyle Boren, on the floor of the House, described the book as "a black, infernal creation of a twisted, distorted mind." Steinbeck was elected to the National Institute of Arts and Letters and also received several threats on his life. The novel was awarded a Pulitzer Prize and the American Booksellers' Award.

The overwhelming public attention caused him much embarrassment and discomfort. He found that so much of his time was spent being a "writer" that he had no time to write. He did not enjoy being lionized and avoided as many of the obligations thrust upon him as he could. For a short time he escaped with Ricketts on a specimen-collecting trip to the coastal waters north of San Francisco.

In addition to the pressure of publicity, Steinbeck was increasingly disturbed by the imminence of a terrifying global conflict. Partly to ease these pressures and, now that he could afford it, partly to indulge his interest in both Mexico and marine biology, he and Ricketts planned a collecting trip to the Gulf of California. For this purpose they chartered a local sardine boat, the *Western Flyer*, and with a crew of four sailed out of Monterey Bay on March 11, 1940. A week later they rounded the tip of Baja California, Cape San Lucas, and began their collecting. Since Steinbeck's chance meeting with Edward Ricketts in 1930, the two had become great friends, and the writer was able to pursue his amateur interest in biology under expert direction and in congenial, enthusiastic company. In the late thirties the Pacific Biological Laboratories, which was the glamorous name of Ricketts' shoestring operation, had run into financial difficulties. Ricketts had pursued his enterprise of supplying laboratory specimens more as a passionate avocation than a business, being satisfied that it provided him with a few simple material wants and great intellectual stimulation. Steinbeck now became a legal partner in the enterprise, bolstering its finances and sharing its professional responsibilities.

Almost immediately after this expedition, Steinbeck returned to Mexico to work with Herbert Kline, producer and director, writing the script for *The Forgotten Village*, a film about a backward Mexican village. Upon completion of the film in January 1941, he began collaborating with Ed Ricketts on *Sea of Cortez,* based on their collecting trip into the Gulf of California, and this work was completed in August. *Sea of Cortez* is an indispensable book for understanding both the orientation of Steinbeck's thinking and his vital relationship with Ed Ricketts. It is an important watershed in Steinbeck's career, for the day after its publication the Japanese bombed Pearl Harbor, and the entry of the United States into World War II disrupted a life style and literary interests to which he would never return.

Another disruptive force was his consuming love affair with Gwyndolen Conger, an attractive professional singer whom Steinbeck first met in Hollywood in the fall of 1940. The consequent separation from his wife and their divorce in March 1943 caused him intense moral anguish. Carol had done much to encourage her writer husband. She had worked at sundry part-time and temporary jobs to help support them; she typed his manuscripts and through discussions helped to form his ideas and techniques. She provided some of the titles for his novels (e.g., *The Grapes of Wrath*), and entered into the writing of them so completely that sometimes in his letters Steinbeck assured his agents that "we" were doing revisions, and referred to new work as "our" novel. His removal to New York City in the fall of 1941 and his subsequent marriage to Gwyndolen further separated him from his California past.

Steinbeck's eagerness to participate in the war effort led him into a wide variety of activities. Together with Ricketts, he drew up a list of papers written in English by Japanese marine biologists that gave usable data on the reefs, depths, tides, nature of beaches, etc., of Japanese-held islands in the Pacific —information vital to any assault on those islands by sea-borne forces. The military, however, was not impressed. Steinbeck also proposed, directly to President Roosevelt, that properly aged counterfeit money be dropped behind enemy lines to cause inflation and disrupt finances. This idea, too, was rejected, not by the President, but by the Treasury Department. (It was nevertheless used effectively in Europe by the Germans.) For a period Steinbeck wrote broadcasts for the Office of War Information, and later held an appointment as a special consultant to the Secretary of War. His talents as a writer were used in *Bombs Away: The Story of a Bomber Team*, published in 1942, a one hundred eighty-four page book liberally illustrated with photographs and designed to entice young men into the Air Force. Another quite different literary effort was *The Moon Is Down*, published the same year, written at the suggestion of the Office of Strategic Services as an encouragement to resistance movements in Nazi-occupied countries. For this work, after the war, he was awarded the Liberty Cross by King Haakon VII of Norway. Finally, in the spring of 1943 he took a position as a war correspondent for the New York *Herald Tribune*, and from June until October he was abroad, stationed first with a Flying Fortress group in England, then in North Africa, and finally with the American forces in Italy, having landed with the assault troops. On his return he wrote the film stories for two motion pictures using war materials—

Lifeboat (Twentieth Century-Fox, 1944) and *A Medal for Benny* (Paramount, 1945). It should be noted that the stock comedy portrait of the Negro in *Lifeboat* and the slurs against organized labor were not part of Steinbeck's original script, and that he objected vigorously to them to the extent of requesting that his name be withdrawn from the screen credits.

The period between 1941 and 1948 was a prolific one for Steinbeck. In addition to the writing directly related to World War II, he published *A Russian Journal* (1947), an account of his travels in Russia with the photographer Robert Capa, and three varied and interesting works of fiction: *Cannery Row* (1945), *The Pearl* (1947), and *The Wayward Bus* (1947). In recognition of his growing stature, Steinbeck was elected in 1948 to the American Academy of Arts and Letters. But that year was also to bring tragedy and mark the beginning of his last phase as a writer. On May eleventh Ed Ricketts, driving across the Southern Pacific tracks, was struck by the San Francisco express; four days later he died. The effect of his life and death on Steinbeck's work is of the first importance. Some indication of the closeness between the two men can be seen in the long essay "About Ed Ricketts," with which Steinbeck prefaced *The Log from the Sea of Cortez* (1951). Thus a final door was closing on Steinbeck's California period. Although he was still to make some attempts at "going home" to California, especially in the two years between his second and third marriages, he was never again able to feel comfortable there.

In 1948, also, his bitter and painful divorce from his second

Outward from California [23]

wife, Gwyndolen, the mother of his two children—Thom,
1944, and John, 1946—left him in a serious psychological
depression that lifted only upon his friendship with and, in
December 1950, marriage to Elaine Scott. During the two
intervening years he had felt grave doubts about his ability to
be a good husband. His great dependence on his third wife's
love and companionship are recorded in *The Journal of a Novel*
(1969), where her devotion to him is clearly seen to be the
sustaining force behind *East of Eden* (1952). Some of his
anguish can be perceived in the Cain and Abel theme of that
novel, and its portrait of the evil Kathy; also in the lesson
learned by Joe Saul in *Burning Bright* (1950) and the small
boy's sense of rejection in the short story "His Father." The
most interesting work of this period between his last two marriages is his film story and screen play *Viva Zapata!* (Twentieth
Century-Fox, 1950), an outstanding motion picture.

In the last sixteen years of his life, Steinbeck devoted much
of his time to travel and living abroad, out of which came a
good deal of poor journalism and only three novels, two of
them slight. In 1952 he traveled extensively in Europe and
published his observations in *Collier's* and various journals. In
1955 he was writing editorials for the *Saturday Review*. Again
in 1957 he went to Europe and pursued his long-standing
interest in Malory and possibly undiscovered material relevant
to the *Morte d'Arthur*, which had so influenced his own work
and sensibility. The following year he again returned to England in pursuit of Arthur, conferring with Dr. Eugène

Vinaver, one of the great authorities on that literature. In 1959 he lived for eleven months in Somerset, working now on a modern English version of the *Morte d'Arthur*. There also he enjoyed the company of Adlai Stevenson, whose two presidential campaigns he had publicly supported, for whom he had written campaign speeches, and whom he greatly admired. Other political figures whom he admired and with whom he had a personal relationship were President Kennedy and, especially, President Johnson, who was a frequent recipient of Steinbeck's advice—solicited or volunteered—and who seemed to enjoy the writer's company at the White House and Camp David.

A year after Steinbeck's return from England to New York, he set off in a camper truck on a three-month tour of his own country, gathering material for *Travels With Charley* (1962). In 1961 he was again in Europe. It was the year of his first heart attack and of his last novel, *The Winter of Our Discontent*. The following year Steinbeck was awarded the Nobel Prize. In 1963 he participated in a cultural exchange that took him on a tour of the Iron Curtain countries. In 1965 there were more trips to England and France, and in 1966 Steinbeck began his "Letters to Alicia" for *Newsday*, an assignment that was to take him not only back to Europe but to Israel and Southeast Asia, including a stay of two months in South Vietnam. He returned from this last trip in May 1967.

In addition to the numerous articles and "letters" of this period, his nonfiction includes the collection of war correspondence he had written in 1943, published under the title *Once There Was a War* (1958), for which he wrote an introduction. *Travels With Charley* (1962) is probably the best-known work of this period, a personal survey of America which was followed in 1966 by *America and Americans*. For the student of Steinbeck's novels, perhaps the most interesting piece of nonfiction was published posthumously in 1969—*The Journal of a Novel*. This account of the writing of *East of Eden* contains startling insights into the diminishing talent that Steinbeck was able to deploy in the writing of fiction.

Ironically, it was the later fiction, together with his journalism and observations on America, that brought him the greatest popularity of his career. *Sweet Thursday* (1954) was turned into a musical, *Pipe Dream*, by Rodgers and Hammerstein. The film made from *East of Eden* was a great popular success. *The Short Reign of Pippin IV* (1957) was a Book of the Month Club selection, and *The Winter of Our Discontent* (1961) was the keystone of his Nobel Prize award the following year. There were other awards and honors: an O. Henry Award, a Paperback of the Year Award, a John F. Kennedy Memorial Library trusteeship, a Press Medal of Freedom, and a Presidential Medal of Freedom. Meanwhile, such earlier works as his short stories and *Of Mice and Men*, as well as *Travels With Charley*, were being produced for television. When Steinbeck died quietly in his sleep on December 20, 1968, it seemed more like the passing away of a public personality than the tragic loss of a great writer.

2

✳✳✳✳✳✳✳

Cup of Gold
and
To a God Unknown:
THE INDIVIDUAL QUEST

OF MANY writers of fiction, it might be said that they failed
to live up to the promise of excellence contained in their first
novels; of others, that they equaled but never surpassed their
first achievements; and of yet a third group, that their earliest
published efforts were but the unsure beginnings of later major
accomplishment. Although it is impossible to foretell a writer's
future performance from his first novel, it is sometimes easy
enough to look back on the career of an established author and
find in that early book the seeds of his future work. John
Steinbeck is such a writer, and *Cup of Gold* is such a novel.

The historical romance is not a form noted for its serious

achievements. The cover of a paperback edition of *Cup of Gold* promises the reader the tale of a "swashbuckling buccaneer—a bold and daring pirate whose bloody deeds struck terror into the proud heart of Imperial Spain." But in place of this purple promise the original edition carried a subtitle: "A Life of Sir Henry Morgan, *Buccaneer*, with Occasional Reference to History." In the comic juxtaposition of this subtitle lies a hint that the book should not be taken seriously as the biography of "a bold and daring pirate." Surely it is evident from the many little details of life in the seventeenth century and from the fact that the major events in the book are those of Morgan's actual life that Steinbeck had done more than "occasional" research in the period. But it becomes increasingly clear as the novel unfolds that the life of this pirate is merely an appropriate vehicle to carry the author's meaning, a meaning which, ironically, is diametrically opposed to the superficial values embodied by its protagonist. Steinbeck's novel examines the adventuring, striving romantic hero and finds him a pathetic, even a ridiculous figure.

This examination is explicitly presented twice, at the beginning and at the end of the book, by two different persons— Merlin, the legendary wizard who appears in the Arthurian stories, and the historical John Evelyn, advisor to Charles II, whose *Diary* Steinbeck may have used as one of his sources. Merlin's reaction in the first chapter to the fifteen-year-old Henry Morgan's burning desire to be off to the West Indies and make his fortune states this theme nicely: ". . . it is very likely that you will become a great man—if only you remain a little child. All the world's great have been little boys who wanted the moon. . . . But if one grows to a man's mind, that mind must see that it cannot have the moon and would not want it if it could. . . ." John Evelyn, in the last chapter, after all the conquests, puts it more succinctly in his reply to the king's surprised observation (about Morgan) "that such a great soldier can be such a great fool": "If great men were not fools, the world would have been destroyed long ago. How could it be otherwise? Folly and distorted vision are the foundations of greatness."

Between these two statements of the novel's theme lie all the trappings of a pirate novel, including the lovely woman held for ransom. As an adolescent, Morgan is exploited by a sailor who sells him in the West Indies as an indentured servant. Four long years he nurses his dreams of becoming a buccaneer, meanwhile reading avidly in his kind master's library about ancient battles and otherwise preparing himself for a career of piracy afloat. This includes not only mastering the art of seamanship, but also the cold, calculating use of other human beings—whether they be his master, his lover, or the slaves in his charge. Morgan is extremely successful on his very first venture, in which he captures four Spanish ships along the Gulf of Darien. He becomes second in command to the Dutch pirate Edward Mansveldt, who is later killed by the Spaniards, leaving Morgan at the head of a large pirate horde whom he leads on one successful expedition after another—seizing treasure galleons, looting towns. He caps his career with the sacking of the quasi-fabled city of Panama, the "Cup of Gold," filled with the treasure of the New World. This last act against Spain, although officially frowned upon, together with some liberal gifts procures him a knighthood, the lieutenant governorship of the island of Jamaica, and his respectable cousin as a bride. In his new official capacity he mercilessly hangs his former associates. He himself eventually dies quietly in bed. This main outline closely follows the biography of the historical Henry Morgan. Morgan's career as a pirate (1660–1685), his seizure of treasure galleons and the sacking of such towns as Porto Bello, Trujillo, and others, was a significant part of the competition, sometimes breaking out into open war, between Spain and England for control of the New World trade.

That all his accomplishments are as ashes in the mouth of the novel's protagonist is clear, and the reader, remembering Merlin's words, comes to expect the increasing disappointment that Morgan experiences. The life of adventure and worldly accomplishments is not ultimately satisfying.

If the novel rested on this level of narration, it might be dismissed as sophomoric. But even in this first work, bearing so many marks of the novice that its author would wish seven years later that it had never been published, we find in essence most of the techniques and themes that will appear in more complex and integrated form in all Steinbeck's major works. At once the most important yet subtle of these techniques is the use of some myth, legend, or literary prototype as the substructure for his fiction. In *Cup of Gold*, this substructure is provided by the *Faust* legend, with an important twist. Like Faust, Morgan in effect sells his soul (his very real talents, knowledge, intelligence) for progressively grander worldly accomplishments, only to find them, each in turn, unsatisfying. But whereas, in the most famous version of the legend, Goethe has his hero finally turn to accepting the very struggle for achievement as an end in itself, finding there his true happiness, Steinbeck's Henry Morgan is deprived of even this consolation. On his deathbed he experiences a fantasy in which all his deeds approach him in the form of "faceless little creatures" and insistently demand, "Why did you do me?" He has no answer; but the recoiling and disappearance of these creatures before the specter of his childhood sweetheart symbolize what has been implicit all along—that these worldly deeds mask an inner failure and sense of inferiority.

The first manifestation of this sense of inferiority is seen in the embarrassment that prevents his meeting with his childhood sweetheart, Elizabeth, the night before he sails for the New World. At the age of fifteen his sense of shame and embarrassment because of his sexual fantasies about Elizabeth are normal enough, but his inability to grow from this point and mature in his personal relations is evident in all his subsequent actions and is in fact the cause of his restless striving. He names the first ship he commands *Elizabeth*, and the lovingness with which he regards her and the tenderness of his helmsmanship—"the strong dear touch of a lover's fingers"—

make it quite clear that the ship is a surrogate for his lost sweetheart. His last conquest—the destruction of Panama—is spurred not by his desire for its gold, but by his desire to prove himself to the world by possessing the beautiful, almost legendary woman of that city, who is known as *La Santa Roja* and desired by all men. Ironically, her real name turns out to be Ysobel (a variant of Elizabeth), and although she had been quite willing to be swept away by the equally legendary buccaneer, Captain Henry Morgan, she sees the real Morgan as a child, scorns him, and gives him his most stinging defeat. In a brilliant paradigm of the novel's theme, he sells this woman whom he cannot possess for still more gold. Carrying the irony yet further, Steinbeck has Morgan retire to the conventional life of a public official, badgered and henpecked by a very dull wife, whose name is—yes, Elizabeth. Accompanying this progression of real Elizabeths is the increasingly romantic exaggeration that his childhood affair takes as Morgan recalls it on four different occasions, so that finally the original Elizabeth is remembered as "a princess of France" and his passionate paramour. The Freudian cast of Oedipus complex, overcompensation, sublimation, and so on, with which Steinbeck embellishes his Faustian theme is so ubiquitous that even Morgan's mother is named Elizabeth.

Although the Faust legend seems to be the most important point of reference in *Cup of Gold*, and it is used ironically to criticize traditional romantic values, Steinbeck also weaves into the fabric of the book many allusions to other legends and myths that parallel his novel in part. Among these are some precise similarities to Ibsen's *Peer Gynt* (especially the ending) and to the legends about the Holy Grail and the quest for the chalice from which Christ and his disciples drank at the Last Supper, and which can be found only by the purest knight. The latter, like the Faust theme, is used ironically. Panama, the treasure city known as "the Cup of Gold," is thus itself a kind of Grail symbol, but this profane cup of gold contains a Red Saint, *La Santa Roja*, whom Morgan fails to possess, thus symbolically failing to attain his worldly Grail. Again Steinbeck constructs a paradigm of this failure in Morgan's discovery, among the loot, of a real gold cup, curiously inscribed with a frieze of four lambs; but these lambs are "grotesque," and the cup is a false Grail, for inside, Morgan discovers and is mocked by a naked girl with arms lifted "in sensual ecstasy."

The various allusions and symbols pertinent to these materials, as well as some allusions to the Fall of Troy through Helen and the yearly journey of the sun god, are nicely woven into the text, so that they complement one another and create a rich texture. Steinbeck skillfully brings in his references with such devices as Morgan's own casual surmise that Ysobel might be "as jealously guarded as was Helen," and Merlin's reminder to the boy Morgan that Britons are the legendary descendants of noble Trojans. The narrative language itself is liberally sprinkled with symbols and images pertaining to these references, such as historical place and proper names, images of roundness, femaleness, coins, towers, sexuality, gold, darkness, light, and the like.

This sensitivity to language in his first novel, in addition to his extensive use of myth and legend, clearly indicates Steinbeck's future course. He never developed a prose style that would mark him as definitely as Ernest Hemingway, F. Scott Fitzgerald, and Thomas Wolfe were marked by theirs. Instead, his prose is distinctly tailored so that it becomes an integral part of the unique quality of each novel. In *Cup of Gold,* this tailoring is grossly obvious and not particularly effective. Limited by the historical surface of his plot and setting, Steinbeck tries to create not only in his speakers but even in his own narrative style a sense and flavor of the period. Perhaps any such effort to recreate a historical speech, especially of a period so rich and distinctive in its own imagery and idiom as the seventeenth century, is foredoomed to failure. It is almost bound to sound like an imitation at best and at worst a parody. The important thing here, however, is this evidence of the young writer's awareness and use of prose style as a variable and purposefully shaped instrument. Triumphs of language as various as *Tortilla Flat* and *The Grapes of Wrath* were yet in the future.

Finally, for the student interested in the development of Steinbeck's resources and strategies as a writer, there can be noted in this first novel the beginnings of a device that was to share with his use of prototypal sources and manipulable language the central importance in his mature work: the biological metaphor, his tendency to explain human motives, desires, actions, in terms of biology. In *Cup of Gold,* this is but scarcely evident, in such casual explanations as that the boy Morgan's yearning to leave Wales for the New World is "a desire for a thing he could not name. Perhaps the same force moved him which collected the birds into exploring parties and made the animals sniff upwind for the scent of winter." The deterioration of survival skills among the overly secure inhabitants of Panama similarly recalls a biological observation. The beginnings of his group-man theory, so essential to *In Dubious Battle* seven years later, is apparent in an officer's observation of his troop of horsemen as "multi-members of one great body governed by his brain."

This first novel is interesting also in terms of Steinbeck's philosophical concerns in his major fiction. Certain characters here symbolize ideas that will recur and be developed later. Among them is Merlin, original of many subsequent "hermit" and seer figures in Steinbeck's work; James Flower, ineffectual recluse from society; the mother of Coeur de Gris (Morgan's lieutenant), practical yet kindly prostitute; and both Elizabeth Morgans, each a competent, unimaginative wife.

In general, this first novel can be seen as the initial exploration of two subjects that would continue to occupy Steinbeck in much of his later fiction. One of these is the contrast between dream and reality, as we have seen above. The other is the contrast between escape and commitment as two approaches to the relationship between the individual and society. *Cup of Gold* does not present either of these approaches; but through Henry Morgan, Steinbeck examines and rejects the validity of individual heroic accomplishment within society. Thus the way is prepared for such extensive examinations of individual commitment to society as *The Grapes of Wrath* and such philosophical positions of escape as *Cannery Row.* Much of Steinbeck's later work swings between the presentation of these two extremes.

Cup of Gold is not a great first novel, but it is definitely not the work of a literary hack. In it, Steinbeck displays an ambitious grasp of subject matter and a vigorous interest in craft that give promise of the technical and philosophical achievements of his best work.

To a God Unknown

To understand clearly the early beginning from which Steinbeck took his direction, it is necessary to consider at this point not his next published book, *The Pastures of Heaven,* which appeared in 1932, but the novel on which he had worked for about five years, and which had failed to find a publisher under two titles and in several different versions. Finally, early in 1933, he sent to his agents *To a God Unknown,* and it was published that fall, just a year after *The Pastures of Heaven.*

Whereas Steinbeck's first novel, *Cup of Gold,* however allusive to archetypal legend, explores, and rejects, the alternative of heroic, individualistic action in a materialistic world, *To a God Unknown* points itself in the opposite direction—the individual's religious submission to whatever power he conceives to order his universe. The pattern of polar alternation (whether physical and spiritual, action and inaction, dream and reality, escape and commitment), established by these two early novels and continued in his major work, makes evident that the early Steinbeck was a serious artist and not merely a writer of entertainments. With some of the faults but also the enthusiasm of an amateur, he was addressing himself to the major question: How does one live?

Although *To a God Unknown* is set in modern times (at the turn of the century) and has as its characters not legendary historical figures but men from the most basic walk of life—farming, the raising of crops and livestock—it soon becomes apparent that ultimately this book has even less to do with agriculture than *Cup of Gold* has to do with buccaneering. Again the surface story is a simple one. Hungering for land, Joseph Wayne, at the age of thirty-five, unmarried, leaves his small farm in Vermont, his father and three brothers, and comes to California, where he establishes a homestead of a hundred and sixty acres. Shortly afterward, upon his father's death, he is joined by his brothers—Thomas and Burton, who are older and married, and Benjamin, who is younger and unmarried. They each claim adjacent homesteads and join with Joseph in working them together as one large holding. For a few years they prosper; Joseph marries and has a child. Then comes a period of drought in which all their labor is destroyed, and Joseph's wife dies in an accident.

Joseph's climactic act of suicide is, however, connected primarily not to his wife's death and the economic losses they suffer in this simple story, but to the pervasive theme embodied in the symbolic landscape and events, and his increasingly pantheistic beliefs and practices. In contrast to *Cup of Gold* which depends for its depth on general allusions to the Faust legend, with a few scattered references to such materials as *Peer Gynt* and the Holy Grail, this new novel combines several sources in greater detail and complexity. Also, while the language of *To a God Unknown* avoids the false archaisms of the earlier novel, the descriptions of scene and action are more replete with symbolic details. Thus, in its main thrust, this new novel is far more clearly nonrealistic.

To begin with, the novel has as epigraph a Vedic hymn. Steinbeck somewhat freely uses as the title for this hymn (addressed originally simply "to whom?") the phrase "To a God Unknown," from which the novel ostensibly takes its title, perhaps derived from the hymn's refrain, "Who is He to whom we shall offer our sacrifice?" Thus the hymn, which is in praise of the creator of all things, the "God over Gods," presumes no knowledge of who this creator is. Interestingly, Steinbeck's version differs from the standard translations in one important respect. They render one of the concluding sentences as a request, a prayer, but Steinbeck uses it as a question—"May He not hurt us, He who made the earth/Who made the sky and the shining sea?"—thus considerably altering the hymn's meaning. This epigraph, together with the name of one of the characters (Rama, wife of Thomas) and the novel's title, indicates one area of the novel's reference, the monistic and pantheistic philosophy based on the ancient sacred literature of Hinduism.

But the novel's title points also to another religious area— Christianity. For, as recorded in Acts 17:22–29, Saint Paul found among the Athenians an altar inscribed TO THE UN-KNOWN GOD and proceeded to enlighten them: "Whom therefore ye ignorantly worship, him declare I unto you. God that made the world and all things, seeing that he is Lord of heaven and earth, dwelleth not in temples made with hands; neither is worshipped with men's hands, as though he needed anything. . . ." It is important to notice that the apostle here is speaking not of Jesus and Christianity but of "God that made the world and all things." This reference to Paul is especially interesting in view of the fact that one of the novel's earlier titles was "To an Unknown God." Thus, although the title points toward two very different religions, these overlap in the similar contexts with which they provide the phrase. Before the novel's action begins therefore, its theme seems clearly indicated: What is the nature of the God "to whom we shall offer sacrifice" and what is the proper worship of Him who "dwelleth not in temples made with hands"?

This balance between Hindu-pantheistic and Christian-anthropomorphic myths is nicely reflected in the name of the valley that provides the novel's major setting—*Nuestra Señora* (Our Lady), named by the early Spanish settlers in honor of Mary, the mother of Christ. As the novel progresses, it clearly develops the suggestion that Our Lady is not so much the

Christian Virgin as the pantheistic Earth Mother herself, source of countless primitive and pagan deities. This is manifested in several ways. For example, immediately after Joseph returns from recording his homestead, he is overcome by the lush, sensuous beauty of his land, "as a young man is who slips out to a rendezvous with a wise and beautiful woman." Succumbing to the female symbolism of "the forest of Our Lady," the "curious femaleness about the interlacing boughs and twigs, about the long green cavern cut by the river . . .," he throws himself face-down upon the ground and "his thighs beat heavily on the earth" in an obvious sexual release. The language of the whole passage is not only erotic but religious as well, describing the forest in terms of a cathedral ("aisles and alcoves"). This passage returns to mind near the end of the novel when, after the death of Joseph's wife, Elizabeth, Rama comes to him in the night. "Their bodies met furiously, thighs pounding and beating. . . . her broad hips drummed against him . . . and her hungry limbs drew irresistibly the agonizing seed of his body." Rama's symbolic role as an incarnation of the Hindu god Vishnu, the Preserver, is emphasized by the mother imagery with which her attentions to Thomas are described; for, as each of the Wayne brothers represents some "answer" to the question posed by the novel's title, Thomas personifies man on the animal level, prior to any need for a god to worship. Fittingly, shortly after their sexual union, Joseph gives Rama the only child of his marriage to Elizabeth, saying, "This child is yours. I swear it now. He is yours forever."

This balancing of pantheism and Christianity is evident throughout the novel. Joseph's brother Burton, a militant Protestant, represents the extremes of Christian opposition to the world, the flesh, and what he calls "devil worship." He is characterized as having "embraced" his wife but four times, celibacy being a "natural" state for him. His face is drawn, his eyes hungry for satisfactions the earth cannot provide. He looks with great suspicion and fear not only on paganism of any sort, but on physical pleasures in general and even upon any different form of Christianity. After a fiesta, during which he witnesses such "evils" as drinking, dancing, and the Roman Catholic priest kneeling to "wooden idols," Burton finds it necessary to go to the camp-meeting town of Pacific Grove for three weeks. He returns so exalted and full of enthusiasm for the fine evangelical preaching he has heard that he soon moves there permanently.

The Catholic priest in the novel, Father Angelo, although also opposed to paganism, is a much more generous and open person. At the fiesta he takes a cup of wine, enjoys the dancing, and even looks on approvingly when Joseph pours on the ground the first cup of wine to be drawn. He is a well-read man and understands the symbolic importance of such an action. Even at the close of the book, when the drought is over and the people dance, naked or costumed in animal skins in the mud, ending in a mass sexual orgy to celebrate the rain, he does not interfere. He starts to, but feels pity for their great need, remembers that his church is wise; confession and atonement are possible. He does speak, albeit softly, when he sees Joseph making a libation to an old oak tree, cautioning him· to "be careful of the groves," and reminding him that "Jesus is a better saviour than a hamadryad." Similarly, he refuses Joseph's request that he pray for the "dying" earth, reminding him that God cares only for the souls of men.

In contrast to the Christianity of Burton and Father Angelo is Joseph's pantheism. This begins as a mere whim that his dead father's spirit has somehow come to be with him, the son who received the patriarchal blessing. But his veneration for his father merges with his attachment for the old oak tree under whose protective limbs he builds his home, and he is soon engaging in simple forms of ancestor worship. From this point, and especially after the drought becomes severe, Joseph's seeking for the Unknown God and his proper worship becomes more and more pagan and pantheistic. It is as if he has ransacked Sir James Frazer's *The Golden Bough*—which absorbed Steinbeck as a college student—for fertility rites and myths, sacrifices, totems, and symbols. His explorations take him into such forms as the Attis and Adonis cults of the yearly renewed god, Druidic practices, divine kingship, sun worship, and animal sacrifice. Joseph himself moves from simple propitiation to a sense of responsibility for the fertility of his land and finally, as he sacrifices himself on the altar rock, to an identification with the earth itself, through which he becomes a manifestation of the life force.

To Joseph's growing obsession with the land's fertility,

Steinbeck subordinates almost every character and scene. Like the older brothers Burton (Protestantism) with his repressed wife and Thomas (prereligious man) with his wife Rama (Earth Mother), the younger brother, Benjamin, also plays his part in the symbolic drama. On a simple level, he clearly represents atheistic modern man, devoted to the pleasures of the world, recognizing no spiritual need. But the indulgence with which the others accept his irresponsible hedonism, his symbolic deflowering—in a dream—of Elizabeth, who is to be Joseph's wife, his murder on the day Joseph brings her home as his bride, and the acceptance of his death as a matter of course all point to another function. He personifies the mock king, discussed in *The Golden Bough*, who was appointed to reign briefly before the new king, or at the beginning of the year, was indulged in every whim, and then murdered as a propitiatory sacrifice for the successful reign of the true king. Even such minor characters as old Romas, Willie, Juanito, and Elizabeth's father contribute in some way to the mystic vision that imbues the surface pastoral simplicity of the novel.

And as each character is used, so is each event and scene, whether it be a sentence or two—the description of a strange bull discovered in the pine grove, a hawk pouncing on a rabbit, Willie's recurrent nightmare—or the most sustained of these descriptions—the wedding journey of Joseph and his wife through the mountain pass. The landscape of this journey is rife with sexual symbolism—the monolith, the cleft, the hidden valley beyond—which make of it a rite of passage from the old to a new life. Related to this use of landscape as a symbolic device is another form of description in which the landscape is rendered as a living being. This occurs frequently, and is not always so obvious as in the scene discussed above in which Joseph "possesses" his land. There are numerous occasions when the landscape is described in female terms as "voluptuous," the dark sage covering the hills is seen as "coarse fur," and the water scars as "saddle sores." The rock in the pinegrove is the land's "heart," and the stream which flows from it is its "life blood." During the drought the land is described as a "picked carcass," a "sick person," a "dead body," a "sleeping" thing; "everywhere the bones of the earth stuck through"; the mountains seem "unfleshed." The height of this metaphoric language is reached near the end of the book when Joseph imagines the land as "vindictive," the hills "like blind snakes with frayed and peeling skins, lying in wait. . . ." He even fears that the land "like a dog far gone in hunger" may turn and attack him.

Conversely, animals and human beings are frequently described in terms of landscape. The jutting hip of a dead cow is viewed as "a mountain peak, and its ribs were the long water scars on the hillsides." Joseph sees his hand as "a mountain range extended in a long curve and on its end were five little ranges, stretching out with narrow valleys between them," an image that is elaborated on for several sentences. This metaphorical fusion of living beings with the earth itself, an important aspect of the book's theme, comes to a climax when

Joseph, during his sacrificial suicide, sees in a vision his body becoming part of the earth, the sky, the rain, and dies content in the knowledge that "the grass will grow out of me in a little while."

As thus in Joseph are reconciled biology and landscape, life and nonlife, so also are the opposites of paganism and Christianity. Although his own religious instincts impel him to make himself responsible for the land's fertility through various pagan rites and rituals, Joseph is tolerant of different expressions of religiosity, such as those of Father Angelo, Burton, and even of its total lack in Thomas and Benjamin. But beyond this he himself is clearly a Christ figure. Early in the novel, he is described in a shaft of light with his arms outspread, and a cock is heard to crow; variations of this crucifixion image occur three times in the course of the novel, including even a Calvary scene with three crosses. During their wedding, Elizabeth twice has the distinct impression that her bridegroom's face is that of Christ. At different times Rama, Juanito, and even Father Angelo also have the same impression. Joseph's self-sacrifice on the altar rock, arms outstretched, is therefore, a Christlike atonement to the offended "father" who has placed a drought on the valley, as well as being a fertility ritual.

Finally, and perhaps most obviously, as indicated by the names Joseph and Benjamin, to some extent the events of the novel roughly parallel the Old Testament story of Joseph and his brethren. It is Joseph who, while not the eldest, receives the patriarchal sign of approval. There are a number of brothers, of whom Benjamin is the youngest, and there is a hint of quarreling among them before Joseph leaves for California. Also, as in the Bible story, dreams are used to predict lean years. But at this point the Old Testament parallels end, and Joseph "saves" his brothers by becoming the Jesus of the New Testament.

To a God Unknown is interesting to the student of Steinbeck for the considerable advance it demonstrates in his craft, as well as for revealing a serious ambition and one of his polar themes. The sureness with which he is able to juggle the various levels of allusion and symbolism is impressive. More important, he demonstrates a true novelist's ability to project an entire, privately created world and make it credible. Considering the strange characters, theme, and action of the novel, this is a considerable accomplishment.

3

❋❋❋❋❋❋❋

The Pastures of Heaven
and
Tortilla Flat:
EXPERIMENTS IN COMMUNITY

CUP OF GOLD, Steinbeck's first published novel, and *To a God Unknown,* which he wrote immediately afterward, are primarily concerned with dynamic individuals whose social environments are depicted only to the extent necessary to provide a background for their actions. In *The Pastures of Heaven* (1932) and *Tortilla Flat* (1935), Steinbeck's focus widens to encompass whole communities; and these two communities differ as much from each other as do the respective protagonists of the two previous novels. As a corollary, whereas each of the first two novels develops a precisely formulated theme, the central themes in the next two books are amorphous; and whereas the earlier works are organized by a closely knit narrative line, *The*

Pastures of Heaven and *Tortilla Flat* are sprawling and episodic.

This abrupt change in direction was to be characteristic of Steinbeck as a writer and the cause of much misunderstanding among his later critics, who assumed that such changes betokened not a fresh, inquiring, experimental talent, but—amazingly—a lack of necessary intellectual rigor and technical competence. At the time that *The Pastures of Heaven* and *Tortilla Flat* were published, however, Steinbeck had not yet achieved sufficient recognition to raise much critical expectations of him as a writer, and thus early comments on the books did not mention a lack of consistency as one of his weaknesses. In fact, *The Pastures of Heaven*, while it sold poorly, was well received by reviewers, who noted its author's "development" in creating greater social and psychological realism in his characters.

Although *The Pastures of Heaven* is usually listed as one of Steinbeck's novels, it comes close to being a collection of short stories unified by a common locale and certain recurrent characters. Thus it compares closely with Sherwood Anderson's *Winesburg, Ohio* (1919), which was quite possibly an influence in these and other respects as well. As in its predecessor, the quite separate episodes of *The Pastures of Heaven* are further unified by a loosely defined common theme. Both books also make use of a "frame story," within which the individual narratives are contained, but by which they are not substantially affected.

Nevertheless, although *The Pastures of Heaven* is probably

the most loosely knit of any of Steinbeck's novels, it is more profitably approached as a whole rather than as a series of separate short stories. It is made up of nine episodes, each of which is concerned with a single individual or family, and, in addition to the framing story, these episodes are bracketed by an opening and closing section not immediately related to any events in the stories themselves but serving, initially, to direct our expectations and, finally, to provide a general commentary.

The stories themselves, all concerned with residents of a valley called the Pastures of Heaven, vary considerably in their leading characters and events, presented in the following order: "Shark" Wicks, who encourages his neighbors' belief in his financial successes, but whose stock-market investments are actually make-believe, until under ironic circumstances he is forced into admitting his real poverty and pretense; Tularecito, a strange foundling of remarkable gifts, who must be committed to an institution for the criminally insane as the result of an action provoked by a well-intentioned teacher; Helen Van Deventer, who perpetuates her masochistic grieving and guilt over her dead husband by killing her insane daughter; Junius Maltby, who has left his job in the city and leads a bucolic life of indolent study and reflection until good neighbors show him the error of his ways and he returns to the city; Rosa and Maria, two sisters, who are happy and make others so by giving their favors to customers who patronize their restaurant, until some idle gossip forces them to leave the valley and support themselves as prostitutes; Molly Morgan, the valley's schoolteacher, who leaves her comfortable situation because she is afraid that the alcoholic bum who has shown up in the valley may turn out to be her father; Raymond Banks, who occasionally serves as an official witness at state executions so that he can visit with his old friend the warden until a morbid neighbor poisons his mind with the gruesome possibilities of bungled hangings; Pat Humbert, who finally comes out of the shell into which he retreated on the death of his parents, but is almost immediately forced back into it when the girl in whom he becomes interested turns out to be engaged; John Whiteside, whose plans for establishing the continuity of his family in an ancestral home are destroyed when his son leaves for the city with his new wife and the house itself burns to the ground.

Such are the disappointments and minor tragedies of the inhabitants of this valley. But Steinbeck's concern is neither with the significance of these rural lives in themselves nor with revelations of the buried life lying beneath the surface of this normal and average farming community. Rather, through the characters he traces a variety of themes that appear in all or nearly all of the stories. The most obvious of these, occurring structurally in each of the stories, is thematically the least important and is established before the individual stories themselves begin, in the second chapter, which gives the history of the Battle farm in the valley. The Munroes are the most recent of three families to live on that farm. Both of the other families had failed to make a success of the farm, and the Munroes themselves arrive there with a background of ill fortune. After a period of initial prosperity, Bert Munroe jokingly suggests that perhaps the farm's curse and his own have "killed each other off," but the rest of the community, with whom the reader is likely to agree, believes that perhaps the two curses have "mated" and that there will be "a lot of baby curses crawling around the Pastures the first thing we know." In this way the suggestion of a curse or ill fortune operates early in the book—as did Merlin's prophecy in *Cup of Gold* and the "blessing" received by Joseph in *To a God Unknown*—to create expectancy in the reader.

It soon appears that the curses have indeed "mated," and the Munroes become agents of the progeny. In the nine stories that follow, it is always the intervention of a Munroe that precipitates the crucial turning point in the lives of the characters—Maltby's return to the city, Rosa and Maria's becoming prostitutes, Tularecito's incarceration, and so on. In no case is this intervention deliberately malicious. Only once, in the Raymond Banks story, is it even self-serving; usually it is well intentioned—as, for example, Bert Munroe's neighborly visit to the Van Deventers, or Mrs. Munroe's gift of clothing to Robbie.

Thus irony is the prevailing tone. The book opens with an account of the valley's discovery in the eighteenth century by a Spanish corporal returning some escaped Indians, who had abandoned "the true faith," to slave labor and repentance at the mission. This disciplinarian, who has "whipped brown backs to tatters," is so affected by the beauty of the hidden valley that he reverently takes off his steel helmet and whispers, "Holy Mother. Here are the green pastures of Heaven to which our Lord leadeth us." The name remains long after the death of the corporal, who with "sentimental wistfulness" had always intended to return here for a little time of peace before he died; instead he dies locked up in a barn of the syphilis that he contracted from an Indian. After ten chapters describing the misfortunes of others who hoped to find peace in this valley, the book ends with another "discovery" of the valley. A busload of tourists looks down on the beautiful valley, and each sees it as a place in which to find peace, an escape from the frustrations of everyday life. Even the bus driver, who makes a point of the valley's name—the Pastures of Heaven—would like to settle down there, seduced by the thought of "how quiet and easy" a man could live.

The irony of the book's opening and closing chapters is reinforced by the second and penultimate chapters, which are part of contemporary life in the valley, and also serve as that life's real beginning and ending. It is in the second chapter, after having given the history of the Battle farm on which the Munroes settle, that Steinbeck brings them to the valley and establishes them in the community. The events of this history make the farm seem cursed and haunted, and are replete with little ironies, such as the fanatic religiosity and inherited madness of John Battle, who covered his clothes with white cross-stitch to ward off evil and who was killed by a rattlesnake that struck him three times in the throat, "where there were no crosses to protect him." The penultimate chapter, too, has its little ironies, in addition to the major one of Bert Munroe's intervention. The little whirlwind, for example, that picks up a spark, carries it into the cellar of the Whiteside home, causing the house's destruction and John Whiteside to leave the valley, neatly balances the little whirlwind that, two generations earlier, Richard Whiteside had taken as a sign of where to establish his house. Structurally this chapter rounds out the book's episodes by having the leading family abandon the valley, the ultimate fulfillment of the curse suggested in the second chapter, and by presenting in epitome the valley's history —its promise and its curse.

While irony is the dominant mode and the intervention of the Munroe family provides the book with its most obvious structural device, there remains the question of theme. The operation of a vague curse does not seem adequate to this purpose. Looking more closely, it becomes apparent that although no clearly defined single theme controls all the stories, a pattern does emerge. In each case a Munroe's intrusion causes a climactic change in the characters' lives by serving, however innocently, as the instrument that shatters some dream or illusion which had provided these lives with order and purpose. In some stories, such as the ones about Shark Wicks and John Whiteside, this theme is worked out simply and directly; in others, such as those about Helen Van Deventer and Pat Humbert, it is complicated by other factors that make a judgment about the change in these lives difficult; finally, in the stories about Tularecito, Junius Maltby, and others, the Munroes themselves serve merely to precipitate a climactic action by the whole community. But within these limits, each story can be seen to illustrate the same general theme: human happiness and fulfillment are tenuous; it is a condition so frail that it can be shattered even by good intentions.

By means of the book's title (which is also, of course, the name of its locale) and the doubly paired opening and closing framing chapters (one, two; eleven, twelve) this theme is amplified by unmistakable allusions to the Garden of Eden. As in Christian myth the creation of the Garden was consequent to the fall of the angels, so the valley is discovered as the result of some Indians who "abandoned religion" and used "diabolic guile" in their escape. The Indians are next discovered, somewhat like Milton's fallen angels at the beginning of *Paradise Lost*, "practicing abominations" at the bottom of a canyon. The coincidence that twenty Indians escaped and that the valley is settled by "twenty families" seems to merge the fallen angels with mankind. These suggestions that the Pastures of Heaven is to be taken as a version of the Garden of Eden are reinforced throughout the novel by numerous references to gardens, gardening, and fruit, for which the valley is famous— a fact repeated in the framing chapters. The expressed opinion in the opening and closing chapters by the Spanish corporal and the tourists (neither of whom enter the valley) that it represents the hope of an idyllic, peaceful existence also contributes to this idea. Furthermore, the Garden of Eden itself is discussed by Junius Maltby and Jacob in one of the stories. Like Steinbeck's use of myth in his previous novels, these references show imaginative and creative variations from the originals. For just as clearly as the Pastures of Heaven is a type of Eden, it is at the same time the world after the fall of man —*east* of Eden, as Steinbeck calls it in a later novel. The second chapter identifies the curious curse that hangs over the valley to be original sin, for John Battle discovers a large snake that he knows is "the damned serpent" and "devil." The novel, then, affirms the Christian view of man as laboring under original sin. Another indication of this double reference is the fact that the valley is discovered in 1776, the date of the signing of the Declaration of Independence. Steinbeck was very probably aware that our early religious settlers looked upon this virgin continent as a "New Eden," another chance, together with forces of evil in the forms of wilderness and wild Indians. Thus, the book also may be taken as a comment upon the earliest form of the American Dream.

The Pastures of Heaven demonstrates again that Steinbeck does not write merely realistic fiction. His habit as a writer is always, whether dealing with the adventures of an individual or the history of a community, to provide for his realistic surface a broad foundation of mythic reference.

TORTILLA FLAT

Steinbeck's next novel, *Tortilla Flat* (1935), continues both his interest in the life of a single community and his technique of structuring that life on a framework of mythic reference. Also continued, perhaps by the very nature of the novel's subject, is the episodic structure. But where the earlier novel relies on two pairs of bracketing chapters to give it architectural form, in *Tortilla Flat* a majority of the episodes themselves are manipulated so as to achieve an organic design having its own natural rise, climax, and dénouement. In other words, *Tortilla Flat* shows a considerable advance in Steinbeck's ability to shape his presentation of a whole community, and points toward his next three novels—the peak achievements of his career. Another advance demonstrated in the novel, and for his future work undoubtedly the most important, is his ability to give this community a distinct identity or group character.

The novel's setting is Monterey, California, particularly its ethnic ghetto, which is given the fictitious name of "Tortilla Flat." Its major characters are what used to be called paisanos, now known as chicanos. The story line is very slight. Danny, returning from World War I, finds himself heir to an old house that becomes domicile, base of operations, and spiritual center for himself and the circle of friends he gathers about him— Pilon, Pablo, Jesus Maria, Big Joe Portagee, the Pirate. The group flourishes for a while, sharing a marginal existence and participating in a variety of unrelated adventures—courtships, thefts, good deeds, swindles—and then dissolves after the death of Danny.

Although in most of the episodes Danny and his friends are central, in others they are only peripherally involved or even serve merely as observers, narrators, and commentators. Their

relaxed, indolent way of life gives them the leisure to become
shrewd onlookers and agile, interestingly unconventional mor-
alists of the scene, who delight in their own speculations on the
vanity of human wishes. Nor do they lack aesthetic interests;
they deliver several pronouncements on the art of fiction: "The
story was gradually taking shape. Pilon liked it this way. It
ruined a story to have it all come out quickly. The good story
lay in half-told things which must be filled in out of the hearer's
own experience." Of another narrative, the didactic Pilon complains, "It is not a good story. There are too many meanings
and too many lessons in it. Some of those lessons are opposite.
There is not a story to take into your head. It proves nothing."
To this, his friend Pablo, belonging to another school of criticism (Impressionism?), replies: "I like it because it hasn't any
meaning you can see, and still it does seem to mean something,
I can't tell what." In such passages, and perhaps in the fish-
throwing episode that follows the discussion between Pilon and
Pilar, Steinbeck is surely using his characters to comment on
the novel itself.

These little excursions into criticism occur naturally in the
lives of these paisanos, who, having no pressing business of
their own, have time to take pleasure in the business of others.
"There were few things going on in Tortilla Flat that Pilon did
not know." But this gossip knowledge does not stay idly in their
minds anymore than do their own experiences. As Pilon puts
it, "Things that happen are of no importance. But from everything that happens there is a lesson to be learned." These

"lessons" are sometimes wonderfully absurd, as when from the fire which, through their own carelessness, destroys their home they learn "never to leave wine in a house overnight." Others are quite subtle, as is the lesson from Danny's gift of a vacuum cleaner to Cornelia Ruiz, whose house does not yet have electricity: "By this we learn that a present, especially to a lady, should have no quality that will require a further present." Still other lessons, such as that deriving from the gift of a small pig, demonstrate how it is possible to receive from a gift somewhat contradictory satisfactions—affection, love, revenge (when it bites you), and finally food. There is often a beautiful satire in these observations beginning, "By this we learn. . . ."

The indolence that provides the leisure for this contemplative life is itself very attractively presented, as in this description of a typical morning: "They did not awaken quickly, nor fling about nor shock their systems with any sudden movement. No, they arose from slumber as gently as a soap bubble floats out from its pipe. . . . Gradually their wills coagulated. They built a fire and boiled some tea and drank it from fruit jars, and at last they settled in the sun of the porch. The flaming flies made halos about their heads. Life took shape about them, the shape of yesterday and of tomorrow." It is this relaxation that makes possible Danny's admirably calm reaction when Pilon brings him the news that one of his houses is burning down. "Is the fire department there?" he asks. And on hearing that it is, he replies, "Well, if the fire department can't do anything about it, what does Pilon expect me to do?" With this he returns calmly to his interrupted business in the bedroom of Mrs. Morales. Despite the aid and comfort of companions, however, Danny cannot remain contented for long with simple security. Unlike his Anglo counterparts in respectable Monterey, he has no worldly goals and ambitions to preserve him from boredom. He turns to violent experience, finally achieving peace in his own destruction.

In the fate of Danny there is an implied criticism of our Western society, or even an observation on the nature of man, which, though here couched in burlesque comedy, Steinbeck is to repeat quite seriously in such major fiction as *The Grapes of Wrath* and the extended philosophical essay *Sea of Cortez*. In fact, there is hardly an aspect of *Tortilla Flat* that does not hold a critical mirror to conventional American society, a world that is conspicuously absent in the novel except in brief glimpses: the stranger in front of the San Carlos Hotel who puts a dollar into Pilon's hand, commanding, "Run down and get four bottles of ginger-ale. The hotel is out"; the "fat ladies in whose eyes lay the weariness and wisdom one sees so often in the eyes of pigs," who are "trundled in overpowered motorcars toward tea and gin fizzes at the Hotel Del Monte"; but most especially the Mexican corporal, who, although himself a victim, accedes to the predatory structure of society, abandoning the principle of honor for that of profit. Another criticism of modern society is implicit in the paisanos' frequent sequences of elaborate rationalization to make the most selfish of motives seem altruistic, a rationalization, however, that is honestly and openly admired and practiced as an art in itself, and not the covert hypocrisy it remains in respectable society. Similarly the paisanos' participation in social rituals, when necessary, is also viewed as a game, rather than the serious affair that respectable society makes it out to be; or, like their role in Danny's funeral, is made into a burlesque of social conventions.

Steinbeck made his final comment on these paisanos ten years after the book was published, in the script he wrote for the film *A Medal for Benny* (1945). There an illiterate paisano during the ceremony when he is being presented with his son's posthumous medal for bravery during World War II, and seeing how commercial interests have exploited and vulgarized the occasion, says, "Benny was a wild boy, but even *Benny* would not do a thing like this. . . . Never would he use the bravery and a beautiful medal to sell a lot of hot dogs and real estate. . . . No—even Benny would not do that." It is fitting that one of the major episodes in *Tortilla Flat* alludes to the life of Saint Francis. Through the character known only as the Pirate, whose life of poverty and dedication to that saint culminates in a holy vision (granted to his dogs!), Steinbeck presents an idealized, although comic, alternative to the materialistic and complicated values of conventional society. This alternative, to a lesser extent, is exemplified by the other paisanos as well. Whereas the citizens of respectable Monterey pile up earthly treasure, which "moth and rust do corrupt," the residents of Tortilla Flat are content to live as Jesus said, like the lilies of the field. In this state of innocence, Pilon, too, has a revelation, while he is absorbed in the beauty of a sunset: "Our Father who art in Nature."

It is not Steinbeck's method, however, to entrust his formal content to such casual allusions. Rather, he uses as his organic principle and controlling base of reference one of the most popular and enduring embodiments of Christian values—the Arthurian legends. This scheme is made clear for the reader in the preface, which in a mock scholarly tone suggests that by "Danny's house" the reader should understand not simply a physical structure, but "a unit of which the parts are men," for this house "was not unlike the Round Table and Danny's friends were not unlike the knights of it." And indeed once this comparison is accepted in the playful way it is obviously intended, parallels appear everywhere—from the initial gathering, growth, and final dissolution of the two groups, and such extended concerns as the search for the Holy Grail (buried treasure), to personal resemblances (Danny, Arthur; the Pirate, Percival) and similarities of incident (the Siege Perilous and Danny's bed; the mysterious deaths of Arthur and Danny). Not that Steinbeck is merely transposing Malory's *Morte d'Arthur* into a modern, and degraded, setting; for like most modern writers, from James Joyce to John Updike, who have incorporated myth and legend in their work, Steinbeck insists on the freedom to shift his correspondences into new and sometimes inconsistent patterns. Thus Danny is usually Arthur but again Launcelot, who is also represented by Pilon; both Jesus Maria and the Pirate are Galahad or Percival. In asserting this freedom, Steinbeck is also repeating the methods of Malory himself, who collected legends of the past, reshaped them, and created figures for them.

From the novel's preface to its last words—"and no two walked together"—Steinbeck's use of Arthurian materials is clear, though perhaps not as obvious as he himself thought. His deep interest in Arthur had started in childhood and continued throughout his life, during the last years of which he immersed himself in a serious and scholarly study of Malory and his sources. (At the time of his death he was working on his own rendition of the *Morte d'Arthur*, which was published posthumously [1976].) He thought of this Arthurian material as having "an enormous effect not only on our literature but on our mores and our ways of thinking about things." Of course, any comparison works in both directions, and although *Tortilla Flat* is a burlesque form in which the parallels to legendary heroic deeds are the root of much humor, these parallels also suggest that perhaps King Arthur's knights had their share of human foibles, and that behind their "heroic" deeds lay sometimes a pettiness now obscured by time. Nevertheless, Steinbeck has too much respect for these old materials to treat them as outrageously as did Mark Twain in his *A Connecticut Yankee in King Arthur's Court*. He also suggests, however humorously, quite explicitly that in time the antics of these Monterey paisanos may also be elevated to those of legendary heroes—Arthur, Roland, Robin Hood.

In *Tortilla Flat* the successful melding of paisanos and the knights of the Round Table is an accomplishment of Steinbeck's protean style. For one thing it is the language which, quite apart from the explicit statements in the preface, keeps the reader aware of the novel's basic ground. The chapter titles, through their imitation of Malory's archaic rhetoric, are the most obvious. For example, chapter one, *"How Danny, home from the wars, found himself an heir, and how he swore to protect the helpless";* or chapter eight, *"How Danny's friends sought mystic treasure on Saint Andrew's Eve. How Pilon found it and later how a pair of serge trousers changed ownership twice.* For those readers familiar with the Arthurian tales, there is suggested in the latter chapter title the beautifully comic movement from the original's Holy Grail to a geodetic survey marker, the only "treasure" Pilon and Big Joe find; from noble knights to paisanos; from a precious suit of armor to a pair of ill-fitting serge trousers. This function of prose style and reference appears also in the paisanos' curious, elevated formal speech and in the intrusions of the narrator as well, so that the defining tone is continually sustained. The importance of this continuity can be illustrated by the failure of the play and the motion picture based on the book, because they were unable to incorporate the narrative prose. Undoubtedly, it was this masterful control of tone, and perhaps its comic nature, that made *Tortilla Flat* Steinbeck's first commercially successful novel.

4

In Dubious Battle and *Of Mice and Men:*

THE MACROCOSM AND THE MICROCOSM

A WRITER of less serious intention than Steinbeck might have hearkened to the ring of the cash register and tried to continue the success of *Tortilla Flat* with another novel in the same warm, whimsical vein. But, counter to the commercially shrewd advice of his friend and editor, Pascal Covici, Steinbeck insisted on having *In Dubious Battle,* a cold, violent book published next. He said he wanted no tag, "humorist or otherwise," on his work. Despite essential differences between these two books, however, there is a certain common denominator —the author's continued interest in the underdogs of a predatory, commercialized society. The scene is changed, from small town to the farms—or rather, in Carey McWilliams' phrase for the nature of California agriculture, to "factories in the field."

Steinbeck acquired his knowledge of the novel's migrant workers and labor organizers as naturally as he had become conversant with the paisanos of Tortilla Flat. His hometown of Salinas, in the heart of a rich lettuce-growing region, had been the scene of much labor agitation, and Steinbeck himself had frequently worked in the fields and listened to the arguments of Communist Party organizers. Everything in the book, from the workers' vernacular, dress, and social behavior to the details of the landscape, is based on personal familiarity. The main incidents of the novel are taken from an actual strike that occurred near Fresno a few years earlier, and the strategies of leadership and organization are based on the actual tactics of two Communists who worked the area. In fact, parts of the book were originally written by Steinbeck in the form of a biographical sketch of such an organizer. This intimate familiarity with his materials made it possible for the author to achieve a realism as precise as a documentary and yet as natural as experience.

The novel's action begins with Jim Nolan joining "the Party" and being sent shortly afterward into the fields with the organizer Mac as his mentor. Arriving at the migrant workers' campsite, Mac uses every means to gain their confidence— even to the extent of delivering a baby. He and Jim then exploit the migrant workers' dissatisfaction with a wage cut to organize a strike, using London, the migrants' natural leader; Dakin, who owns a good truck; Sam, the most violent striker; and Burke, who turns out to be an informer, as lieutenants. The strikers are also assisted by Anderson, a small grower who lets them camp on his property; Doc Burton, an uncommitted observer and commentator who directs the legally required sanitation arrangements; and Joy and Dick, fellow Communist party members. The strikers' confrontation with the three powerful growers who employ them is violent and, in the face of superior strength and the law, doomed to failure.

The risk of Steinbeck's close familiarity with such material lay in the possibility of his precommitment and prejudice in the presentation; but he was fully aware of this danger and was able to avoid it. He said it was not his purpose to look through "the narrow glass of political or economic preconception." This is not to say that he was without any preconceptions whatsoever —he firmly believed that every migrant worker should be humanely treated and not irresponsibly exploited. As author, his stance toward the novel is close to that of Doc Burton, one of its characters, toward the strike situation: that of an open-minded observer whose involvement transcends the particular and immediate terms of what is taken as a conflict of universal forces—"the whole thing."

This objectivity permeates every aspect of the book, from action, scene, and character to prose style and symbolic structure. For example, not one of the numerous specific details about the strikers is flattering; almost all are pejorative. Steinbeck knew that it would defeat his purpose to elicit pity and sympathy through pathetic characters and scenes (à la Dickens); that, assuming the reader's disposition toward fair play and human dignity, he needed to develop some qualifications in order to achieve a fair picture. This is significantly evident from the very first migrant worker we meet, a bully who refuses to share some paper scraps for bedding. It continues to be evident in the sullen young apple picker who negligently bruises the fruit and threatens a company employee with violence when advised to be more careful. The men who are assigned the job of protecting Anderson's house and barn, in simple return for his permission to camp on the property, thus making it possible to carry on the strike, neglect their obligation and cause his ruin. The occasional glimpses of dirty personal habits, unfounded suspiciousness, and pointless cruelties serve the same function of undercutting our natural sympathies for the strikers. Even their leaders—Dakin, Burke and London —share these qualities. The cause may be just, but it does not therefore follow that its proponents are personally admirable.

Conversely, although the growers' cause is patently unjust, both the "Super" and the only owner whom we meet—briefly, when the two come to the workers' camp—are impressive for their personal courage and dignity under pressure. The blatant injustice of the owners' ways of dealing with the strike is counterweighed by the strikers' own methods, and ironically both Dakin and London assert that if *they* owned the orchards, the first thing they would do would be to have the strike's organizers ambushed and shot.

A third major force in the novel, presented with the same intricate balance, is the Communist party itself—never thus explicitly named but obviously so identified. There is no other force on the scene that is so capable of helping the workers resist dehumanization and achieve fair wages. But although Mac and Jim, the party's organizers, are accepted by the strike leaders, it is only for their superior knowledge of tactics. The mass of workers must be kept ignorant of the party's presence, for like most American workers they are suspicious of "Reds." Furthermore, although the party may help the workers achieve their immediate goals, it becomes obvious that its real purpose is to train the workers as a revolutionary force, to be exploited eventually toward an end far more ambitious than a raise of five cents an hour in wages. And the means which the party organizers employ are as unscrupulous and inhumane as those of the owners. Yet even this larger purpose, although concealed from the workers, is never presented as mere political ambition, but always as an idealistic commitment to establishing a more just distribution of material goods and opportunity for human development.

This impartial conception of the book's various materials ("cold" and "brutal," Steinbeck called it) is implemented by the prose style. Although the speech of the men is forcefully rendered and full of picturesque folk metaphor, the prose of the narrative is flat and colorless, never attracting attention to itself, always objective like a fixed camera, indifferently recording from the same location with the same light a cheap boarding-house room or an apple orchard, the birth of a baby or the smashing of a face. Steinbeck once said that he had always had a stronger feeling for the "texture" of a story than for its characters or theme. This is well illustrated by *In Dubious Battle*, in which every aspect is presented in the same sharp, hard-grained prose. It is Steinbeck's most objective novel, clearly a masterpiece of the realist-naturalist school, an accomplishment all the more admirable in that he never indulges the panoramic view, but limits all the action to the angle of vision of Jim, the book's most engaged character. Undoubtedly it was this very realism and objectivity, complexly established, that caused critics and reviewers of strong political persuasion, of both the Left and the Right, to overlook the work's very real artistic accomplishments. Steinbeck was disappointed that the book was largely taken as a tract rather than a novel.

If the picture of the novel thus far presented seems a static one, it is because this picture is the product of a long and abstract view. Up close and in particular, this stasis is the resolution of reciprocally balancing forces of great mass and energy, each itself the product of many separate vectors. The novel opens with one man sitting alone in a quiet furnished room and it ends with that same man dead, his face blown off by a shotgun blast, his body propped up above a crowd of perhaps a thousand men, being used to whip them into a vindictive mob that will almost certainly be butchered by a superior force of well-armed, equally bloodthirsty deputies and vigilantes. The pacing of the action that leads to this conclusion is brilliant. The opening movement is slow and expansive as it introduces the forces or themes and develops them together to the point at which an old worker, Dan, falls out of a tree. This precipitates the strike, and from that point on, with well-spaced moments of dramatic stillness, the novel builds in tempo and intensity to its implied conclusion—a great symphony in which the final chord, the massacre of the strikers, is not sounded, but heard clearly in the imagination.

The mutual relationship between Mac and Jim and their relationship to the workers is an important part of the novel's subject. Only through these relationships does Steinbeck bring the book's vast forces down to the level of individual humanity. Through Mac and Jim as mentor and neophyte, Steinbeck makes easy and natural an elucidation of the labor organizers' goals and methods; through their different personalities he explores the cause and nature of commitment. This relationship is kept from becoming static by the two men's changing posture not only toward each other, but also toward situations which they themselves have largely engineered.

In the beginning it is Mac who seems cruel and dehumanized in his single-minded devotion to the party's long-range goals. The destruction of a sympathizer's lunch wagon, the death by fire of two beautiful dogs, the delivery of a baby (without adequate knowledge)—all are object lessons to illustrate that "we gotta use everything," even the bodies of dead comrades, to win over the workers. In this dedication there is no room for outside attachments: "Don't you go liking people,

Jim. We can't waste time liking people"; and "There's no such things as personal feelings in this crowd. Can't be." Even Jim's gazing up at the stars elicits from Mac a terse "You look at the road." Mac is not utterly devoid of feelings, but he has learned to submerge them through his devotion to the cause. Before the novel's end, however, Jim in this respect surpasses his teacher. Like Mac, he never loses his essential humanity, as is evident in his desire, shortly before his death, just to sit in an orchard and watch things like ants and new green leaves, and is especially evident in his visits with Lisa and the baby. But he grows beyond Mac in a dedication to the cause that amounts to a martyr complex. "Use me," he keeps urging his mentor. "I want to be used." Furthermore, it becomes increasingly evident that whereas Mac acts from knowledge and experience, Jim acts through the sheer inspiration of one touched by a holy fire. Finally, it is Jim who emerges as the teacher, "going in a straight line" with no deviations, and Mac who by failing to suspend his humanity falls into the very errors against which he has warned his pupil. Thus, ironically, it is almost certain that the destruction toward which Mac incites the workers at the novel's close, while admittedly not for the workers' benefit, is not even for the party's cause, but rather to avenge Jim's death—in other words, for entirely personal reasons.

The conception of the workers as an instrument, a single entity rather than a collection of individuals, is not limited to the party organizers but is shared by various other characters:

Dan, the old worker ("It's like the whole bunch . . . was one man"); London, the migrant workers' leader; and especially Doc Burton, who theorizes extensively about this phenomenon: "A man in a group isn't himself at all, he's a cell in an organism that isn't like him any more than the cells in your body are like you." This "group-man" (as Burton terms it in his further theorizing), which serves as one of the book's major elements, is a far more sophisticated conception than that of Dan or London or Mac or Jim ("just one big animal"). That Burton's ideas reflect those of the novelist is seen clearly through reading *Sea of Cortez* (1941), Steinbeck's collaborative effort with Edward F. Ricketts. There are passages in the latter work that seem to be paraphrases of what Doc Burton says, but stated in more precise biological terms. Steinbeck believed that man, like certain other animals, cannot be understood without taking into account the sometimes "herd" nature of his actions and motivations. But however much the striking workers of *In Dubious Battle* gave Steinbeck the opportunity to experiment with using an aggregation of individuals as a major force in a novel, and through Doc Burton to theorize about this entity, he uses this conception for a more central artistic purpose.

As the novel's title and epigraph from Milton's *Paradise Lost* clearly indicate, Steinbeck's vision of his materials, as usual, extends from the realistic to the mythic. Milton's epic poem seeks to explain man's fallen condition by tracing it back via Christian myth to the war in heaven between God, the Son, and the Holy Spirit on the one hand, and on the other rebellious angels who, under the leadership of Lucifer (Satan), sought to wrest power from the Almighty. After the rebels' defeat, and from their new abode in Hell, Satan sets forth to spite God by inciting the newly created Adam and Eve also to rebel through disobedience.

The larger correspondence is apparent. The group of striking workers are the rebellious angels whose leader is Mac, or Mac and Jim together. The three owners of the valley, whose authority they challenge, together make up an omnipotent deity —a three-personed god, two of them with such suggestive names as Hunter and Martin (Mars, god of war). The details of this correspondence are numerous. They include specific resemblances between Satan's cohorts and Mac's delegated leaders: Beelzebub, Satan's closest advisor, is London; Moloch, impatient for attack, is Sam; Mammon, the rebel who succumbs to materialism, is Dakin; there is even a Belial and an Abdiel in Burke and Dick. Resemblances in specific action and scene also exist. With artistic purpose, to suggest that the "dubious battle" (between God and Satan, Good and Evil) is a perpetual one, Steinbeck has his novel end as *Paradise Lost* begins, with a harangue by Satan (Mac) designed to rouse the rebels from their recent defeat to some further action, a harangue in which both Satan and Mac three times hesitate because of their strong, choked-up emotions; the strikers camp reminds us of the Pandemonium built in Hell; the fallen angels' epic games have their counterpart in the pastime activities of the idle strikers. In context, when the strikers are told by Bolter, the owners' chief "archangel," that they are going to be "kicked off this place," that "we blacklist the whole damn bunch of you," and that they will have no place "this side of hell," the expulsion from heaven is clearly intended.

Although Satan's rebellion in heaven is an important element in *Paradise Lost*, a more important concern is "of man's first disobedience and the fruit of that forbidden tree"— Satan's seduction of man from God. *In Dubious Battle* relates these two subjects as did Milton. Thus Mac and Jim as Satan come to the Torgas Valley to manipulate the agricultural workers into rebellion against the three-personed owners of the valley. And this theme, too, is clearly indicated by a series of suggestive details and parallels: the tree in the Garden of Eden becomes a whole orchard of apple trees; some details of Satan's journey to Eden are suggested in the journey of Mac and Jim to the valley; as Satan's success was made possible by Eve, so Mac and Jim succeed because of Lisa, without whose pregnancy they could not have gained the men's confidence. The strike is born with Lisa's baby, and its success or failure is associated with the baby's future.

It may be asked at this point why, if Steinbeck was sympathetic with the workers, did he thus identify them with rebellious angels and fallen man? The answer lies in Milton's own treatment of his subject—the doctrine of the fortunate fall, that through rebellion and "dubious battle" was eventually made possible the achievement of a more noble dispensation for mankind. Although mankind was banished from the physical Garden of Eden, he was in return endowed with an immortal soul. Thus both Satan and the Party are made to serve mankind. In Milton this outcome is seen as God's long-range providence, which of course does not apply to the orchard-owner god of *In Dubious Battle*. Steinbeck may, however, be giving a slight twist to the whole affair and suggesting that capitalism will eventually elevate labor to keep the Communists from winning it over.

The extent to which Steinbeck was conscious of Milton may be surmised by the fact that he put him into his novel in the guise of Doc Burton. The parallels are striking. Like Milton, who sought "to justify the ways of God to man," Doc Burton, unique in the novel, wants to grasp "the whole picture"; Milton's Calvinistic belief in original sin becomes Burton's belief that "man has met and defeated every obstacle, every enemy except one. He cannot win over himself"; and how beautifully ironic it is that whereas Milton was in fact blind but had the vision of divine inspiration, Burton insists, "My senses are . . . all I have. I want to see. . . . I don't want to put on blinders and limit my vision. . . . I want to be able to look. . . ." The number and seriousness of the references to *Paradise Lost* indicate that Steinbeck saw the struggle between labor and capital in epic terms, and considered it to be of the same order of importance as the Biblical myth of man's fall.

The rebellion of Satan and the fall of man serve well enough. But Steinbeck goes further in this direction. Very clearly the

young Communist, Jim Nolan, serves Steinbeck not only as a
Satan figure, the corrupter of mankind, but also as a saviour,
a type of Christ. After all, in one sense Milton's Satan also,
albeit unwittingly, served to enlarge man's moral potential, to
"save" him from the very limited possibilities of remaining an
agricultural worker in the Garden of Eden. The most obvious
device by which Steinbeck endows *J*im (note the initial) with
Christian attributes is through the theme of conversion and
salvation. The novel opens with Jim in his boardinghouse
room, his previous life ("I'd never known any hope") at a dead
end: "I feel dead. Everything in the past is gone." He wants
to "start new," and that he succeeds in breaking through into
a new life after his commitment to the Communist party is
remarked on by others: "You're waking up, Jim. You're looking
better." That he is "born again" is suggested by the fact that
a new name (baptism) is proposed for him. Despite his assertion that he has "no use for religion," the light which is seen
on several occasions in his eyes *is* that of a passionate convert.
He repeatedly begs Mac to "use" him ("Lord, make me an
instrument"). But he is preceded in martyrdom by the older
comrade, Joy, whose mind and body have been broken by
repeated beatings and whose very name suggests the evangelical rapture with which he "preaches" to anyone who will listen.
Mac's eulogy over Joy's dead body amounts to a definition of
martyrdom and applies to Jim as well: "He was greater than
himself. . . . There was a kind of ecstasy in him all the time,
even when they beat him . . . he wasn't afraid." He completes

the definition when he says at the funeral exactly what he later says of Jim: "He didn't want nothing for himself." Moments before his own death, Jim's face is "transfigured. A furious light of energy seemed to shine from it." Thus, after the shotgun blast that kills Jim and obliterates his face but, miraculously, leaves him in a kneeling position, Mac's sharp exclamation, "Oh, Christ," has been well prepared for.

Jim Nolan is but one of many Christ figures in Steinbeck's fiction—from Joseph in *To a God Unknown* to Ethan Allen in his last novel, *The Winter of Our Discontent.* No matter how different their conditions and actions, their lives take on significance by their engaging in the most essential attribute of Christ—sacrificing their lives for the benefit of mankind. Clearly, no reading of this brutal, "realistic" strike novel can be responsible without taking into account its extensive use of Christian myth and Biblical reference. For it is through this means that Steinbeck not only presents his materials, but also evaluates them.

OF MICE AND MEN

The novel that followed *In Dubious Battle,* and which carried its author to a higher level of popular success than had *Tortilla Flat,* seems on all counts a very different accomplishment. Whereas the strike novel explored the dynamics of vast social forces, *Of Mice and Men* addresses itself to what Steinbeck called "the microcosm." Correspondingly, the title is taken not from an epic but from a short pastoral poem by Robert Burns, "To a Mouse, on Turning Her Up in Her Nest, with the Plow, November, 1785": "The best-laid schemes o' mice an' men,/Gang aft agley" (go oft astray). The number of characters is limited to half a dozen, and the book itself is not much longer than one hundred small pages—a novelette.

Of Mice and Men opens with two itinerant ranch hands, making camp in a secluded spot the night before reporting to a new job. George is "small and quick" with "restless eyes," "sharp" features, and ready mind. Lennie is in every way the opposite. George, the obvious leader, is worried that Lennie may again innocently misuse his massive, blundering strength in a harmful way. But the two are tied to each other by the dream they share, of getting a place of their own and finding there security and happiness. At the ranch George shields Lennie from the other hands in situations that might bring out his real nature. The obstreperous Curley, the boss's son, however, insists on bullying Lennie, who finally crushes Curley's hands in his own huge paws. Later Lennie unknowingly breaks the neck of Curley's wife when she panics while he is intending only to stroke her hair. A posse is formed to pursue him, but he is found by George, who shoots him as an act of kindness, to keep him from being lynched by the mob or sentenced to life imprisonment.

Despite this simple plot, *Of Mice and Men* bears important similarities to *In Dubious Battle*. For one thing, both books are nonteleological, or mechanistic, in their point of view. That is to say, the author assumes that there is no final cause or ultimate purpose in the universe. Steinbeck's original title makes this even more explicit—"Something that Happened." Related to this similarity in points of view are their dramatic methods of presentation, including such stage conventions as the unities of time and place. Of course these methods are more pronounced in *Of Mice and Men,* which Steinbeck thought of as an experiment in what he called the "play-novelette" form, a play, he said, "in the physical technique of the novel." Thus each chapter is a different scene, with a brief "stage setting," and with "entrances" and "exits" in narrative form. In fact the novelette was first produced on stage directly from the original pages with very little change necessary.

A more subtle and significant similarity lies in the structure within which the major characters relate to one another. The large group of strikers in *In Dubious Battle* is treated basically as one powerful physical entity, "one big animal"; the massive Lennie of the novelette is insistently described in such terms as "horse" and "bear." And just as Mac and Jim act as the "intelligence" and leaders of the strikers, so George serves as the brains and leader for Lennie. Clearly, Lennie can stand for *all* the workers in the strike novel and George for their leader. On another level, one reinforced by their close and constant togetherness and certain similarities of appearance and body movement stressed in the opening scene, George and Lennie can be viewed as two parts of a single being. They correspond obviously to man's intelligence, or head, and to his physical nature, or body. On a more sophisticated level, Lennie, with his simple and powerful desires ("earth longings" and "inarticulate . . . yearnings of all men," according to the author) represents the Freudian id, and George is clearly its controlling ego. This latter level of correspondence has its parallel, too, in *In Dubious Battle:* Doc Burton's belief that rational man is always and only defeated by something within himself; the id, like Lennie, never learns anything. *Of Mice and Men,* therefore, although lacking the length and epic reference of the strike novel, uses similar materials to achieve a microcosm as impressive as the macrocosm of *In Dubious Battle.*

But while the above complex of meanings form the skeletal substructure of this novelette, what gives the book solidity in the reader's mind and real stature among Steinbeck's works is the empathy created by George and Lennie in their striving to overcome essential human loneliness. The story is set, in the first words of the book, "A few miles south of Soledad," an actual place in California whose Spanish name means both loneliness and a lonely place. In the opening scene, "as though he had said them many times before," George speaks these words: "Guys like us . . . are the loneliest guys in the world. . . . they don't belong no place. . . . They ain't got nothing to look ahead to." This is one aspect of the theme, the constant threat of loneliness; but, as Lennie interjects, with them it is different: *"But not us!* . . . because I got you to look after me, and you got me to look after you. . . ." At the ranch, loneliness is a part of all the workers' lives and is explicitly confessed by

Crooks, the black, crippled stable boy; Candy, the maimed old clean-up man; and even Curley's wife. Perhaps it is because of their own failure to find human companionship that these people, as well as Carlson (another hand) and Slim (the mules-kinner), are suspicious of George and Lennie's closeness and assume that perhaps George is exploiting Lennie. Yet all the ranch hands, from the basis of their own particular loneliness, eventually come to understand how it really is with George and Lennie.

Because as readers we are privileged to see and understand more of the two men than any of the characters can, and perhaps also because we are not lonely ranch hands, we do not have this initial problem. Rather, our difficulty tends to be a more literary one—the inherent sentimentality of such a relationship. The sentimentality, however, is carefully contained by a practical realism. George is not entirely altruistic; he profits from the friendship in several important ways, each of which is illustrated at least once in the story. He has in Lennie the physical protection of great strength and a loyal companion of unquestioning obedience. More subtly, he even has through Lennie a constant boost to his own ego, a reminder of his own superiority, a sense of doing good, and even an excuse for his own failure. This latter advantage is substantiated by George himself when he admits to Slim, "I ain't so bright neither. . . . If I was just a little bit smart, I'd have my own little place, an' I'd be bringin' in my own crops. . . ." Furthermore, while the hope of getting a little farm of their own is the sustaining dream of Lennie, the follow-up to George's frequent "If I didn't have you, Lennie" is a destructive one—"I could take my fifty bucks and . . . cat house all night . . . gallon of whiskey . . . play cards or shoot pool." When we consider that without Lennie, George shows little interest in the sustaining dream, it is clear that Steinbeck is making an observation on the conflicting desire of the id (the body, or mass man) and the ego (the mind, or leader figure).

Another reference that gives greater scope to the simple events of this novelette is the Cain and Abel story, to which Steinbeck was to return for his central metaphor fifteen years later in *East of Eden,* his longest novel. Although George is not literally Lennie's brother, he does act as his keeper, thus fulfilling Cain's question, "Am I my brother's keeper?" A second hint of the Biblical analogue lies in the preponderance of names beginning with *C*—Candy, Crooks, Carlson, Curley, Curley's wife (as she is always known). Furthermore, that there are no names beginning with *A* is in accord with the Biblical account that Abel had no descendants. Correspondingly, the scene is an agricultural one, and the workers, as migrants, fulfill God's "curse from the earth" in the Old Testament: they are fugitives and vagabonds to whom the earth does "not yield her strength." Moreover, each of the *C* characters is in some way, and to varying degrees, a destroyer, even if only of a dream (Crooks) or of a dog (Candy).

Only one of the workers is an exception to this Cain identification—Whit (Wheat?), in whom we see no destructiveness, but who nevertheless is described as if bowed down by a sack of grain and thus figuratively associated with Cain. Of the four people mentioned but not present in the novel, two combine the *A* and *C* initials—Aunt Clara, Andy Cushman. Of the other two, both madams of whorehouses, the bad one is called Clara, but the "better" one, like Whit, has a name without the Cain initial—Suzy.

The names of the three main characters—George, Lennie, Slim—also avoid any use of the initial letters; yet Lennie kills Curley's wife, George kills his "brother," and Slim directs the killing of both Candy's dog and Lennie. Slim, through such attributes as his "understanding beyond thought," "God-like eyes," his "ageless"-ness, and his exercise of irrefutable authority, is clearly a God figure. He directs the necessary killing of Candy's dog, and of Lennie as well, out of love and compassion: the dog is old and suffering; it would be "no good" to have the vicious Curley kill Lennie, or to "lock him up an' strap him down and put him in a cage." George, too, kills out of knowledge and love. As for Lennie, Slim himself observes, "He ain't mean. . . . He's jes' like a kid. . . ." Lennie's killing of Curley's wife, as of the mice and puppies earlier in the book, is done out of some level of love, and in innocence.

The world of *Of Mice and Men* is a fallen one, inhabited by sons of Cain, forever exiled from Eden, the little farm of which they dream. Although in this fallen world, death and violence are the lot of mice and men alike, some men are more innocent than others.

This pervasive allusion to the Cain and Abel story, together with the previously discussed amplification of George and Lennie into such larger terms as, for example, id and ego, would seem quite sufficient means for structuring Steinbeck's little novel. However, it employs at least three other devices which, although less significant, provide further meaning. One of these devices is the constant use of hand imagery. On one level this serves simply as an element of characterization. Thus Lennie's hands are more like "paws"; George has "small, strong hands"; Curley keeps one hand in a glove full of vaseline; Crooks has pink palms; Candy is missing a hand; the hands of Curley's wife are referred to only as fingers and red fingernails; Slim has large, capable hands "delicate in their action as those of a temple dancer." But this use of hand imagery falls far short of accounting for the well over one hundred times that it appears in this short novelette. Steinbeck sometimes seems to go out of the way for an excuse to use the word "hand," or insists on using the word when it is already implied, as in "He carried one small willow stick in his hand." Frequently, hands are seen as almost independent of the person himself: "His [Lennie's] hands went into the pocket again"; "Lennie's closed hand slowly obeyed"; "George . . . looked at his right hand that had thrown the gun away"; "Slim . . . looked down at his hands; he subdued one hand with the other and held it down."

Curiously, the common use of the word "hand" to mean simply a workman, especially on farms and ranches, occurs only once. But perhaps this is the root source of all the hand images.

The lives of the characters are so circumscribed that they are more hands than complete men. Curley is said to be "handy," but Lennie "ain't handy." Yet the incident in which Curley attacks Lennie is described entirely in terms of hands; and, symbolically, it concludes with Curley's hands being crushed in the huge paws of Lennie.

Another kind of device that contributes to the meaning and order of Steinbeck's play-novelette is a use of foreshadowing so persistent as to result in a heavy sense of fate. In the very first scene, when Lennie takes a dead mouse from his pocket, he is reminded by George of the girl he once innocently molested, and he is cautioned about not getting into trouble again, "like you always done before." After George and Lennie arrive at the ranch, these portents are continued. The dead mouse gives way to a dead puppy, the girl to Curley's wife, who is called "jail bait," and Curley himself, who threatens violence at every appearance. There is hardly a page on which one or more of these portents does not appear, and sometimes they are so clustered or follow each other so rapidly that the effect is one of imminent disaster. To them are added two other devices. Particularly effective in a delicate way is George's constant game of solitaire. Less subtle, perhaps too obvious, is the relationship of Candy and his dog, which is made parallel to that of George and Lennie—their first appearance together, the dog following; the length of their association; Candy's concern, yet also his feeling of being trapped in the relationship. Thus the mounting threats to the dog and his eventual shooting foreshadow the destruction of George's "dog," Lennie, which eventually takes place, shot by the same gun in the same way —"right in the back of the head . . . why he'd never know what hit him."

All these devices for ordering and at the same time amplifying the meaning of *Of Mice and Men* are contained within the circular movement suggested by the opening and closing scenes. The action opens at a secluded pool of water, a place of life, to which everything from lizards and rabbits to deer and men come for nourishment, and to whose cavelike thickets George asks Lennie to return "if you jus' happen to get in trouble like you always done before." This pool's suggestiveness as a place to which all life comes in its time is continued in the description of it again in the last scene. But this time the heron who presides over the pool is seen as a predator, feeding upon a little water snake—"A silent head and beak lanced down and plucked it out by the head, and the beak swallowed the little snake while its tail waved frantically." After a brief rush of wind, scurrying of leaves, and a rippling of the pool's surface —a curiously suggestive movement—another small snake is seen swimming toward the waiting heron. And exactly at that moment Lennie appears out of the brush. The profound effect of the novelette's final action, George's shooting here of Lennie, is in part due to the circularity, the sense of completeness which is established on several levels.

Of Mice and Men is a deceptively simple work that can be read sentimentally only by ignoring the depths of reference which underlie its theme of loneliness, a reference that extends even to an allusion to Easter. Soledad, where the novelette takes place, is an abbreviation for "Our Lady of the Loneliness" (as Los Angeles is short for "Our Lady of the Angels"), and thus refers to Mary, the mother of Christ, during that period from Good Friday to the Resurrection on Easter Sunday. Although there is no direct indication of the calendar date, *Of Mice and Men* begins late on a Friday afternoon and ends the following Sunday.

5

The Grapes of Wrath:
AN ACHIEVEMENT OF GENIUS

STEINBECK is frequently identified as a proletarian writer of the nineteen thirties, one whose dominant interest lay in the social and political problems of the Great Depression. But although *In Dubious Battle* and *Of Mice and Men* might generally seem to justify this reputation, neither work is specifically dated either by its materials or by Steinbeck's treatment. Migrant workers and union organizers had long been part of the California scene—and continued so to be. Steinbeck's early short story, "The Raid" (1934), dealing with two labor organizers, similarly avoids identification with its decade. It was not until 1939, at the very end of the period, that he published *The*

Grapes of Wrath, a work clearly and specifically grounded in conditions and events that were then making news. In fact, so directly and powerfully did this novel deal with contemporary events that it itself became an important part of those events —debated in public forums, banned, burned, denounced from pulpits, attacked in pamphlets, and even debated on the floor of Congress. Along with such works as Upton Sinclair's *The Jungle* and Harriet Beecher Stowe's *Uncle Tom's Cabin, The Grapes of Wrath* has achieved a place among those novels that so stirred the American public for a social cause as to have had measurable political impact. Although thus associated with this class of social-protest fiction, *The Grapes of Wrath* continues to be read, not as a piece of literary or social history, but with a sense of emotional involvement and aesthetic discovery. More than any other American novel, it successfully embodies a contemporary social problem of national scope in an artistically viable expression. It is unquestionably John Steinbeck's finest achievement, a work of literary genius.

To appreciate fully this accomplishment, it is important to keep in mind Steinbeck's independence from the extensive literary and political proletarian movements of the period. He took no part in the organized efforts of writers, critics, and scholars to promote leftist or Communist theory as fulfillment of their responsibility to society; nor was he personally committed to any political viewpoint. While this kind of ideological neutrality enabled him to escape the pitfall of being too close to his materials—prejudice and propaganda—Steinbeck's intimate knowledge of his materials contribute greatly to the novel's realism and hence to its authority.

This familiarity had started while he was still a boy working on the farms and ranches surrounding his hometown of Salinas; it had grown through his college years during vacations and drop-out periods. More recently, in the autumn of 1936, he had written an article on migrant labor for *The Nation*, and a series of seven articles on these "Harvest Gypsies" for the *San Francisco News*. Steinbeck's fiction had early shown an absorbing interest in man's relationship to the land. He had explored it in terms of myth and biology in *To a God Unknown*, communally in *The Pastures of Heaven*, and as a factor of maturation in the short stories of *The Red Pony*. But through the field trips he made and the reading he did in preparation for his articles, and through subjecting himself personally to the migrant experience by living and working with the laborers, he was able to extend considerably the range of his terms to include the economic and, in the largest sense, the political. The truth of his observation in these latter dimensions of *The Grapes of Wrath* has long been substantiated by historians, sociologists, and political scientists; the truth of the novel's vision of humanity has been proven again and again in the hearts of its readers.

The novel's main characters are the twelve members of the Joad family: Grampa, Granma, Pa, Ma, their children Winfield, Ruthie, Noah, Al, Tom (just returned from prison), Rosasharn and her husband Connie, and Uncle John, joined by the

ex-preacher Jim Casy. Dispossessed of their Oklahoma homestead by the banks having foreclosed the mortgage on their
property, after the impoverished soil and dust storms made it
impossible for them to support themselves, the group leaves for
California, where they expect to find work as field hands.
Meanwhile their land is joined to that of other unfortunate
neighbors and worked with huge tractors. During the long
journey the Joads find that they are part of a large migration
of people with whom they share dangers and privations—
especially the Wilson family. Grampa and Grandma Joad die,
and Noah leaves the group en route. The rest of them arrive
in California to find the labor market glutted with families like
themselves, resented and disliked by the inhabitants, exploited
mercilessly by the large growers and oppressed by the police.
Connie deserts the family; Jim Casy is arrested, appears later
as a labor organizer but is killed by vigilantes, one of whom is
in return killed by Tom, who then becomes a fugitive; Rosasharn's baby is born dead, and the novel ends with the Joads
and their new friends, the Wainwrights, being even more
hungry, ill, and impoverished than they were at the start.

All the characters are drawn as fully credible human beings,
individual yet also representative of their social class and circumstances. This is true even of such clearly unusual and
strong personalities as Tom Joad, Jim Casy, Ma Joad, and her
daughter Rosasharn. Casy, although a vision-pierced prophet,
retains enough elements of his revival-meeting, "Jesus-jump-
ing" sect and cultural folkways to remain specifically human.

Ma Joad's heroic maternal qualities reflect the strength and character of those migrant wives who not only survived but nourished as well their children and husbands. Steinbeck may have had these women especially in mind when he chose the title "Their Blood Is Strong" for the republication of his *San Francisco News* articles. Such details as Grampa's senility, Al's abilities as an automobile mechanic, Connie's faith in cheap, correspondence trade schools, Uncle John's guilt complex, and Rosasharn's pregnancy personalize each character in turn and contribute to the reader's involvement. But Steinbeck was not writing a novel of personal adventure and misfortune. His theme is the entire social condition of which his characters are a part, and it is primarily in terms of the total situation that they have existence. Thus their role is collective, representational of the Okies and migrant workers, just as in the novel the Shawnee Land and Cattle Company represents the evicting landlords, and the California Farmers' Association represents the growers.

That Steinbeck succeeds in creating characters capable of bearing such wide responsibility is a brilliant achievement, but the novel's vast subject requires even more. To have put the Joads into the large variety of situations needed to add up to a total picture would have destroyed their necessary credibility as particular and real people. Rather than vastly increasing the number of characters and thus weakening the reader's empathetic response and the novel's narrative line, or digressing from the action with authorial comment, Steinbeck conceived the idea of using alternating chapters as a way of filling in the larger picture. About one hundred pages, or one sixth of the book, is devoted to this purpose. At first glance it might seem that putting these digressions from the Joad family into separate chapters interrupts the narrative line even more, and that such a device breaks the book into two distinct parts, or kinds of chapters, resulting in a monotonous tick tock effect. Of this danger the author was well aware, and he avoided it by using in the interchapters a variety of devices to minimize their interruption of the narrative action, temper their expository nature, and otherwise blend the two kinds of chapters in the reader's mind.

Perhaps the most important of the devices Steinbeck uses is dramatization. Chapter five, for example, deals with the process by which mortgaged lands are taken over by the banks, the small farmers evicted, and these lands combined into vast holdings cultivated with efficient modern machinery by absentee landlords. Whereas such previous writers in the naturalist tradition as Theodore Dreiser and Frank Norris would have addressed the reader directly on these points, giving him a well-researched lecture, Steinbeck presents a series of vignettes in which, through generalized characters, situations, and dialogue, we see these things happening. The device is reminiscent of the medieval mystery plays which dramatized Bible stories and made them real to the common people; or of Greek drama which through familiar figures and a chorus of elders or women gave voice to the people's ethical and religious beliefs.

Even the introduction and the transitions between these vignettes share this dramatized quality, as in the opening paragraph of chapter five, in which "owners" are presented walking, talking, touching things, and "tenants" are listening, watching, squatting in the dust which they mark with their little sticks, their wives standing in the doorways, the children wriggling their toes. In similar fashion other chapters present further aspects of the total situation: chapter seven, the buying of used cars for the trip; chapter nine, the selling of household goods; chapters seventeen and twenty-three, the nature of migrant life along the road.

Another device that Steinbeck uses to integrate the two kinds of material is juxtaposition. Of course, everything included in the interchapters is related to the events of the narrative. And each interchapter is so placed that its content is most pertinent to the action in the chapter that precedes or follows it. Highway 66 is the subject of the interchapter that follows the Joads' turning onto that highway; the rain and flood of chapter twenty-nine set the stage for the novel's conclusion. But furthermore, and most effectively, the interchapters are frequently used to develop or complete some specific action initiated in the preceding narrative, or vice versa. Chapter eight ends with the Joads driving off to sell their household goods; the interchapter that follows presents us with generalized characters selling just such goods; in chapter ten the Joads return with the empty truck, having sold their goods, pack the truck, and leave home; chapter eleven describes the gradual deterioration of an abandoned house. A variation of this device is achieved by repetition, in which some specific detail in one kind of chapter reappears in the other, thus further knitting the two together. The anonymous house in an interchapter becomes the Joad house when, in the following chapter, the latter also is seen with one of its corners knocked off the foundation; the anonymous man with a rifle who in the same interchapter threatens the tractor driver becomes Grampa Joad, who in the next chapter is reported to have shot out the headlight of a tractor.

To temper the expository nature of the interchapters and blend them with the rest, Steinbeck works with the prose style itself. The colorful folk idiom and figurative language used by the Joads, Wilsons, Wainwrights, and other migrants reappear in the dramatizations of the interchapters as the language also of the generalized characters. But (except for a brief oversight in chapter five) the conversation in the interchapters is not marked off by quotation marks, thus emphasizing its generalized nature and at the same time further blending it into other elements in these same chapters, weakening the identity and separateness of the more directly expository passages. Finally, through frequent variations in prose rhythm and idiom specifically pertinent to a particular scene, any tendency to group the expository chapters together as different in kind from the narrative ones is discouraged. Consider, for example, the variety of effects presented by chapter three on the turtle, chapter seven on the selling of used cars, chapter twenty-five on the California harvest.

There is, however, another important element of continuity in the prose style, in addition to the spoken idiom of its generalized characters. From the opening chapter, describing the drought, to the penultimate one, describing the flood with which the novel ends, the syntactical structures and rhythms of the narrative voice are those of the King James Bible: "The tractors had lights shining, for there is no day and night for a tractor and the discs turn the earth in the darkness and they glitter in the daylight." Almost disappearing in some of the chapters and totally possessing others, this voice, through its inescapable association with the Bible, becomes the moral center of the novel. It speaks with the force and authority of an Old Testament prophet, some Jeremiah haranguing a sinful people: "There is a crime here that goes beyond denunciation. There is a sorrow here that weeping cannot symbolize. There is a failure here that topples all our success. The fertile earth, the straight tree rows, the sturdy trunks and the ripe fruit. And children dying of pellagra must die because a profit cannot be taken from an orange."

All this is not to say that the sixteen interchapters are equally brilliant or successful. Perhaps three of them (nineteen, twenty-one, twenty-five), concerned with historical information, and a few paragraphs in two or three others, are too direct. But these are exceptions. For the most part, the problem raised by the use of interchapters is fully met by the brilliance of Steinbeck's literary technique.

In themselves, then, the interchapters accomplish several things for the novel. As has been mentioned, they provide an artistically acceptable place for the author's own statements, and they make possible the inclusion of additional materials without overusing the Joads or introducing many other specific characters. Closely related to this latter function is these chapters' capacity for amplification. They present dramatically with a sense of real experience what would otherwise be left to inference—that the situations and actions of the Joad family are typical of a large group of people, that the Joads are caught up in a problem of national dimensions. These are perhaps the chapters' most important uses. In addition, they provide information—the history of land ownership and migrant labor in California, for example. Also, through their depiction of American people, scenes, and folkways, there emerges the portrait of a substantial portion of a people—their political and religious beliefs, their music, manners, stories, jokes; their essentially pioneer character, with its virtues and its limitations. *The Grapes of Wrath* is a "great American novel" in every sense of that phrase.

The brilliance of conception and technique with which Steinbeck manages the larger units of his novel is equally evident in its small details. This is well illustrated by the migrants' frequent use of animals in their figures of speech, as natural to these people as literary references to professors of English. A tractor pushing over a shed "give her a shake like a dog shakes a rat"; Al, in his sexual pride, behaves like "a dung-hill rooster"; when all the Joads are forced to move into one house, Muley describes them as "piled in John's house like gophers in a winter burrow." Casy, the most intellectual of the Joad group, sometimes elaborates these simple figures of speech in his attempt to understand a new idea or express it to others—as when he envisions the socioeconomic forces in terms of a gila monster with its poison and its unbreakable hold, or compares the plight of the migrants to that of a bird trapped in an attic, trying to escape.

The narrative passages also make use of animals, but tend to employ them symbolically rather than figuratively. At the beginning of their journey the Joads' dog is killed on the highway by a "big swift car" which does not even stop. Another dog, the "lean brown mongrel . . . nervous and flexed to run" who upon sight of strangers "leaped sideways, and fled, ears back, bony tail clamped protectively" symbolizes the conditions of the "Hooverville," a group of cardboard and tin shanties, in which his owner lives. A jackrabbit that gets smashed on the highway, lean gray cats, birds, snakes, and even bugs—all appear under perfectly natural circumstances and yet serve also as symbols. The most extended example of this is the turtle that is accorded the first interchapter entirely to itself. The indomitable life force that drives the turtle, the toughness that allows it to survive predators and trucks, the efficiency of nature that uses the turtle to unwittingly carry seeds and bury them, are clearly characteristic also of the Joads. They, too, carry their house (the truck) with them, survive the natural catastrophe of drought and flood and the intimidations of police and vigilantes; they, too, pick up life in one place and carry it to another. This correspondence is further strengthened when in the very next chapter Tom picks up a turtle as a present for the younger children, talks about turtles with Casy, and eventually releases it to travel—as the Joads are to do—southwest.

Steinbeck's use of machine imagery, though not so extensive, is similarly brilliant. As the first interchapter was devoted to the turtle, so the second is devoted mostly to the tractor, which through its blind power and lack of feeling comes to symbolize the impersonal industrialization and mechanization which, following the economic collapse of their family homestead, is bringing an end to the Joads' old way of life: "The driver . . . could not see the land as it was, he could not smell the land as it smelled; his feet did not stamp the clods or feel the warmth and power of the earth. . . . No man had touched the seed, or lusted for the growth. Men ate what they had not raised, had no connection with the bread. Behind the tractor rolled the shining disks, cutting the earth with blades—not plowing but surgery. . . . the long seeders—twelve curved iron penes erected in the foundry, orgasm set by gears, raping methodically, raping without passion." Not that Steinbeck in this chapter, or in the book, is symbolizing the evils of machinery, but rather the evils of its misuse. "Is a tractor bad? . . . If this tractor were ours it would be good. . . . If our tractor turned the long furrows of our land, it would be good. . . . We could love that tractor then. . . . But this tractor does two things— it turns the land and turns us off the land."

The tractor as symbol of a new era appears almost exclusively in the first part of the book; the most pervasive machine imagery is that of cars and trucks, from the shiny red transport which brings Tom home from prison to the broken-down jalopies of the migrants and the sleek new touring cars of the wealthy and the landowners. As a man used to be judged by the horse he rode, so now his social position is revealed by his car; as a man used to have to know about galls, chipped hooves, curb chains, saddle sores, he now must know about tires, valves, bearings, and spark plugs. "Funny how you fellas can fix a car. Jus' light right in an' fix her," Casy says to Tom and Al. "I couldn't fix no car, not even now when I seen you do it." "Got to grow into her when you're a little kid," Tom said. "It ain't jus' knowin'. It's more'n that." Survival, whether of man or animals, rests upon the ability to adapt to or master the new factors of environment. The Joads have this ability. Even before the moment comes when they are to leave their home, they instinctively gather around the truck that is to carry them to California: "The house was dead, and the fields were dead; but this truck was the active thing, the living principle. . . . This was the new hearth, the living center of the family." From this beginning, through various tire punctures, flickering headlights, and boiling radiators, to the ending, in which "the old cars stood, and water fouled the ignition wires and water fouled the carburetors," the condition of the Joads and their fellow migrants is the condition of their machines.

Powerful and unstinting as these machine images are in their reflection of the Joads' physical condition, there is developed

at the same time a counterthrust which makes the novel a cry
not of despair but of hope and affirmation. This thrust begins
with Casy's early self-questioning and ends with Rosasharn
breastfeeding a starving old man. The migrants journey west
along Highway 66, but also along the unmapped roads of social
change, from an old concept of community lost in the blowing
dust of the opening chapter, or forfeited by foreclosed mort-
gages, to a new and very different sense of community formulated gradually on the new social realities. In an interchapter
(seventeen), Steinbeck gives us this process in the abstract, and
it is detailed in both kinds of chapters throughout the book.

Not all, however, can participate in this process. Muley
Graves (a suggestive name) stays behind in Oklahoma, living
in a cave like an animal because he cannot separate his sense
of community and identity from the land and its history of
personal experiences: "Place where folks live is them folks." As
the generalized migrants in one of the interchapters express it
to the buyers of their household goods, "You are not buying
only junk, you're buying junked lives. . . . How can we live
without our lives? How will we know it's us without our past?"
Grampa Joad, like Muley, cannot bear to leave the land. He
is given an overdose of painkiller and carried off it, but he does
not make it beyond the Oklahoma border. Casy's little funeral
speech assures the folks that "Grampa didn't die tonight. He
died the minute you took 'im off the place. . . . Oh, he was
breathin', but he was dead. He was that place, an' he knowed
it. . . . He's jus' stayin' with the lan'. He couldn't leave it." As

it is expressed in one of the interchapters, "This land, this red land is us; and the flood years and the dust years and the drought years are us."

The old sense of identity and community is invested not only in land and possessions, but in social customs and mores that also must be left behind; for example, traditional male and female roles. Ma Joad may be consulted briefly concerning food and space in the decision to include Casy in the family group, but once that decision is made she goes back to the house and womanly things. It is Casy who takes his place among the planning men grouped around Grampa, whose patriarchal headship must be acknowledged despite his senility. Similarly, when they take their places on the truck, Rosasharn, although pregnant, cannot sit in the cab on a comfortable seat: "This was impossible because she was young and a woman." The traditional distinction in social role is also evident in Ma's embarrassment at Casy's offer to salt down the pork. Ma "stopped her work then and inspected him oddly, as though he suggested a curious thing . . . 'It's women's work,' she said finally." The preacher's reply is significant of many changes to come in the sense of community and the individual's changing role: "It's all work," he says. "They's too much of it to split up to men's or women's work." By the end of the book, the male role, deprived of its breadwinner status, loses also its authority. It is Ma Joad who, as woman and Earth Mother, becomes the nucleus of order and survival.

It is fitting that this break with domestic tradition should be announced by Casy, the spiritual leader of his community. He has already abandoned preaching the hell-fire, blood-of-the-Lamb evangelism which is typified in the book through the recollections of Pa Joad, when the spirit took him, "jumpin' an' yellin' " and Granma "talkin' in tongues." This primitive religion is also dramatically presented in Uncle John's sense of guilt and Mrs. Sandry's frightening of Rosasharn with predictions of the horrible penalties God visits on pregnant women who see a play or do "clutch-an'-hug dancin'." Significantly, during the happiest moment in the book, the dance at the federal migrant camp, "The Jesus-lovers sat and watched, their faces hard and contemptuous. They did not speak to one another, they watched for sin, and their faces condemned the whole proceeding."

Casy's new direction rejects such theological notions of sin ("There ain't no sin and there ain't no virtue. There's just stuff people do."); it defines the religious impulse as human love ("What's this call, this sperit? . . . It's love."); and it identifies the Holy Spirit as the human spirit in all mankind ("Maybe all men got one big soul ever'body's a part of"). Casy joins the migration not to escape or to preach but to learn from the common human experience: "I'm gonna work in the fiel's, in the green fiel's, an' I'm gonna try to learn. . . . why the folks walks in the grass, gonna hear 'em talk, gonna hear 'em sing. Gonna listen to kids eatin' mush. Gonna hear husban' an' wife poundin' the mattress in the night. Gonna eat with 'em an' learn." What Casy finally learns, in jail after giving himself up to save Tom and Floyd, is that man's spiritual brotherhood must express itself in a social unity, which is why he becomes a labor organizer. The grace that he reluctantly says before eating his first breakfast with the Joads is already groping in that direction: "I got to thinkin' how we was holy when we was one thing, an mankin' was holy when it was one thing. An it on'y got unholy when one mis'able little fella got the bit in his teeth an run off his own way, kickin' an' draggin' an' fightin'. Fella like that bust the holiness. But when they're all workin' together, not one fella for another fella, but one fella kind of harnessed to the whole shebang—that's right, that's holy." It is for this belief in a new sense of community that he gives his life, rediscovering for himself his American heritage of Thomas Paine's *The Rights of Man*, Ralph Waldo Emerson's "The Over Soul," Walt Whitman's *Democratic Vistas*.

Although varying considerably in their ability to share Casy's spiritual vision, it is the Joads' growing acceptance of the social application of that vision that gives them and the other migrants their strength to endure and their faith in a better future. Even Muley knows why he must share his stringy wild rabbit with Tom and Casy: "What I mean, if a fella's got somepin to eat an' another fella's hungry—why, the first fella ain't got no choice." Mrs. Wilson's answer to Ma Joad's thanks for help puts it differently: "People needs [have the need] to help." A few pages later, Ma Joad's reply to Mrs. Wilson's thanks for help gives the concept a further turn: "You can't let help go unwanted." It is significant that the first example of spontaneous sharing with strangers on the journey is a symbolic merging of two families: Grampa's death in the Wilsons' tent, his burial in one of their quilts with a page torn from their Bible; Ma Joad's promise to care for Mrs. Wilson. As Pa Joad expresses it later, "We almost got a kin bond." Near the end of the novel, Al Joad tears down the tarpaulin that hangs between themselves and the Wainwrights, so that "the two families in the car were one." In one of the most hauntingly beautiful scenes of the book, a family spontaneously shares their breakfast with a stranger (Tom), and their hard-found paying job as well, even though this shortens the time between themselves and starvation.

Consider in contrast the Joads' neighbor who turned tractor driver: "I got a wife an' my wife's mother. Them people got to eat. Fust an on'y thing I got to think about is my own folks." Ma Joad herself starts out on the journey with a ferocious defense of her own family against all things, because "All we got is the fambly"; four hundred pages later she has learned, "Use' ta be the fambly was first. It ain't so now. It's anybody. Worse off we get, the more we got to do." Tom Joad has learned in prison to mind his own business and to live one day at a time. As he puts it, "I'm just puttin' one foot in front a the other," and again a few pages later, "I ruther jus' lay one foot down in front a the other"; in another image, "I climb fences when I got fences to climb." By the end of the book he says, "But I know now a fella ain't no good alone"; and he goes out dedicated to work for the improvement of his people, though it may mean his own death: "Then it don' matter. Then I'll be ever'where—wherever you look. Wherever there's a fight so hungry people can eat, I'll be there."

These are only a few of the particulars that key into chapter seventeen's more abstract statement: "They shared their lives, their food, and the things they hoped for in the new country. . . . twenty families became one family, the children were the children of all." The family of man is established, the change from "I" to "we," the new sense of identity and community through which the people survive. Those who do not share, who continue selfish and distrustful, "worked at their own doom and did not know it."

Of all the abstract statements, generalized examples, and specific acts addressed to this principle of survival, Steinbeck saved the most powerful for the novel's concluding scene. In Rosasharn's feeding of a stranger with the milk from her own breast is reenacted the primal act of human nourishment and the most intimate expression of human kinship. That the stranger is an old man and that, for physical reasons, Rosasharn is glad to give the milk, which continues to gather painfully in her breast although her baby is dead, make its symbolic assertion all the stronger. The significance of this final act is further magnified by the facts that the old man is weak from giving his share of the food to his son, and that the son had "stoled some bread" for him but the father had "puked it all up." The ultimate nourishment is the sharing of oneself, as Rosasharn symbolizes by literally giving of her body. This act takes on religious overtones by the still, mysterious, and lingering quality of the scene as "her lips came together and smiled mysteriously" (the last words of the novel), suggesting a common subject of religious paintings—the Madonna nursing her child whom she knows to be the Son of God.

These overtones do more than enhance a humanistic symbol, however. They bring to conclusion a whole level of the novel that exists in religious terms beginning with the title itself, *The Grapes of Wrath*, a phrase from "The Battle Hymn of the Republic" that alludes to the Book of Revelation in the Bible, containing prophecies of the coming Apocalypse: "And the angel thrust in his sickle into the earth, and gathered the vine of the earth, and cast it into the great winepress of the wrath of God." The reference is reinforced in one of the novel's interchapters: "In the souls of the people the grapes of wrath are filling and growing heavy, heavy for the vintage." From this beginning, the Biblical allusions follow thick and fast, for Steinbeck enlarges the significance of his Okies' experiences by associating them with those of the Israelites (the chosen people) in the Old Testament and thus suggesting their human and historical importance. Although not formally so divided, the novel falls into three parts: the drought and dispossession (chapters 1–11), the journey (chapters 12–18), and the arrival in California (chapters 19–30). This corresponds respectively to the oppression and bondage of the Israelites in Egypt, their Exodus and wandering in the wilderness, and their entrance into the Land of Canaan. The plagues in Egypt, which released the Israelites, have their parallel in the drought and erosion in Oklahoma; the Egyptian oppressors, in the bank officials; the hostile Canaanites, in the equally hostile Californians. In both accounts the Promised Land is first glimpsed from a mountain top. As there were twelve tribes of Israel, so are there twelve Joads (counting Rosasharn's husband). Even the family name recalls a parallel—the tribe of Judah, or the Jews. Ma Joad's simple faith that "We're the people," is reminiscent of the Jewish faith in God's promise that the Jews are a chosen people, as expressed in Psalm Ninety-five: "For He is the Lord our God; and we are the people of his pasture, and the sheep of his hand." As the Jews formulated new codes of law by which they governed themselves in their Exodus (see the Book of Deuteronomy), so the migrants evolve new codes of conduct (see chapter seventeen). When Uncle John sets Rosasharn's baby in an apple box among the willow stems of a stream, saying, "Go down an' tell 'em," it is the counterpart of Moses in a basket among the bulrushes. A Negro spiritual completes the allusion for the reader: "Let my people go." These are but a scattered sampling of the many, often quite specific parallels through which Steinbeck—in addition to the recurring Biblical prose style mentioned earlier—sustains in the novel a strong religious presence.

The Biblical parallels of three of the novel's characters, however, is of such significance and complexity that they require further discussion—Casy, Tom, and Rosasharn. Jim Casy is, as his initials suggest, in several ways a Christ figure. He breaks from the old religious beliefs and practices, of which he was an advocate, and after a retreat "in the hills, thinkin', almost you might say like Jesus went into the wilderness," emerges to preach an initially unpopular new testament, rejecting a god of vengeance for an oversoul of love. "You can't hold no church with idears like that," Tom tells him. "People would drive you out of the country. . . ." He dedicates himself to establishing his "church" among the people and is killed uttering as his last words a paraphrase of Christ's "They know not what they do": "You don' know what you're a-doin' "; Tom, who has been a doubter all along, now announces himself as Casy's disciple. It all fits together very neatly, too neatly. Steinbeck, however, like other modern American writers, such as Faulkner, is not content to use elements of Christian myth on the simple level of allegory. Thus Casy's Christ role is deliberately confused in two ways. First, he is given attributes of John the Baptist, such as the description of his speech as "a voice out of the ground," and, of course, his role as a baptizer. One of those he clearly remembers baptizing is Tom Joad, and thus the second area of confusion.

For Tom Joad, too, beginning with his baptism by Casy, is given the attributes of a Christ figure. He is even called "Jesus Meek" by his fellow prisoners because of his grandmother's Christmas card with that phrase on it. Once when he seems to be rebelling against his emerging role and says he wants to "go out like Al. . . . get mad like Pa. . . . drunk like Uncle John," his mother shakes her head. "You can't, Tom. I know. I knowed from the time you was a little fella. You can't. They's some folks that's just theirself an' nothin' more. . . . Ever'thing you do is more'n you. . . . You're spoke for." In other words, his succession to the role of Christ the Messiah, or Saviour, is complete when, in a scene rife with womb imagery (mother, cave, food, darkness), Tom is figuratively reborn and tells his mother of his vocation to preach and live the words of Casy. His speech, quoted in small part above (page 106), paraphrases the words of Christ recorded in Luke 4:18 and Matthew 7:3 and 25:35–45, as well as in Isaiah 65:21–22: "And they shall build houses and inhabit them, they shall not build and another inhabit; they shall not plant and another eat." Tom Joad is a complex figure, and it is possible to see in him also sufficient attributes (a specific act of violence, for example) to identify him as a type of Moses who will lead his people to a better future, or the apostle Paul, particularly in the specific details of his conversion.

Though not so rich a figure, Rosasharn also gathers to herself multiple Christian aspects. To begin with, her real name, Rose of Sharon, from the Song of Solomon ("I am the Rose of Sharon, and the lily of the valleys") is frequently interpreted as referring to Christ. The Song of Solomon also contains the line, "This thy stature is like to a palm tree, and thy breasts to clusters of grapes." Thus the final scene in which she feeds the old man with her milk is symbolic of the Eucharist: "Take, eat, this is my body. . . ." Through this identification, the anonymous old man becomes Grampa Joad, whose image for

materials and techniques but each exploring some reaction toward a world whose basic values had plunged it in turn from eleven years of severe economic depression into the massive aggression and destruction of a world war.

In *Cannery Row* (1945) this reaction is one of escape into a counterculture superficially reminiscent of *Tortilla Flat,* except that the earlier novel is a light, tongue-in-cheek affair, and the new novel—for all its humor—is a philosophically based and impassioned celebration of values directly opposed to the capitalist ethic dominant in Western society. Looking through "another peephole," Steinbeck discovers that what normally might be called "thieves, rascals . . . bums" may just as truly be described as "saints and angels and martyrs and holy men." For, as Doc, the central character, expresses it, the traits leading to success in our society are frequently "greed, acquisitiveness, meanness," whereas failure may be the result of "kindness, generosity, openness, honesty, understanding and feeling."

The book is short and episodic, made up of thirty-two little chapters, totaling only 181 pages. The setting is the section of Monterey, California, characterized by its sardine canneries (Cannery Row), and the time is just before World War II. Its numerous and varied characters include Doc, the biologist who runs the one-man Western Biological Laboratory; Dora Flood, madam of the Bear Flag Restaurant (a whorehouse); Lee Chong, owner of a grocery store; Mack and the boys (Hazel, Eddie, Hughie, Jones), who live in a storage shed they call the

Palace Flophouse and Grill; Gay, who lives with the boys or in the jail to escape his wife; Henri, an avant-garde painter; Mr. and Mrs. Malloy, who live in an abandoned boiler; Frankie, a retarded juvenile whom Doc befriends; and many others, some of whom appear briefly. The book's narrative line is a very thin one, consisting of Cannery Row's two attempts to give a surprise party for Doc, whom they all admire. The first one turns out to be a glorious failure, resulting in the wrecking of the laboratory and ending before Doc even arrives. After a period of gloom, a second party is launched and proves a riotous success. The novel closes with Doc washing the dishes the following morning.

Cannery Row offers neither a detailed anatomy of society's "mangled craziness" nor a program for changing it. Rather, it brings into being a new world to replace the one that is in the process of self-destruction. It is a world not of whole cloth, but of bits and pieces, varying in chronology, recollected in nostalgia and lovingly assembled, like the patchwork quilt presented to Doc by the girls of Dora's whorehouse, or one of the fantastic collages done by Henri, the novel's eccentric artist. Thus, while one episode concerns the death of the American humorist Josh Billings (1885), in another, Model T Fords are in common use; while Henri follows "feverishly . . . in periodicals the latest Dadaist movements and schisms," Sam Malloy's historically contemporary Chalmers 1916 piston and connecting rod is valued as a rare antique; elsewhere in the book, the year 1937 is clearly referred to as in the past. In addition to this

free intermingling of various time levels, there is also a haunt-
ing effect of timelessness, achieved in part by the relative lack
of plot (movement) and in part by the recurrence of specific
descriptions and acts. A mysterious old Chinaman goes down
to the sea each evening at five thirty and returns each morning.
The rhythmic flopping of the loose sole on his shoe, normally
a very temporary condition, through its presumed continuance
accentuates that timelessness. These two qualities of the
novel's time sense, its blurring of chronology and the sharp
reoccurring detail, are the very essence of homesickness, out of
which Steinbeck said he wrote the book; his close friend Ed
Ricketts, the original of Doc, described it as "an essay in
loneliness." *Cannery Row* brings together again in the un-
changing world of art those qualities of life that—hastened by
the war—had passed never to return, and for which Steinbeck
felt a deep nostalgia. In this respect, the novel is firmly in the
pastoral tradition.

In the novel's preface, addressing himself to the problem of
setting down Cannery Row "alive," Steinbeck proposes an
analogy that resonates through all aspects of the work, for as
its time sense is in free flux, so also are its other qualities. His
comparison of the writing of this book to capturing whole
fragile and delicate sea worms extends to both content (stories/
sea worms) and method or form ("let the stories crawl in by
themselves"/"ooze by themselves"). And as the seawater in
which the specimens are held has no shape except that im-
parted by its container, so the novel seems equally arbitrary in

form. Only about half of the thirty-two chapters pick up the tenuous narrative thread. Alternating almost regularly with these are "the little inner chapters" (as Steinbeck once called them) that sometimes add to our knowledge of the main characters and sometimes introduce material of no causal relationship. Generally, however, all these inner chapters serve in some way as comment or contrast to the novel's major theme.

The openness and freedom of the novel's structure is a formal expression of those same qualities in the Cannery Row community itself, upon which no convention or authority imposes conformity or direction. It has instead the natural order of a biological organism, manifesting its own inner dynamics. The lines of interaction between individuals and even between institutions proliferate in all directions—Frankie and Doc, the laboratory and the whorehouse, the Chinese grocery store and the Palace Flophouse, the idealized women in Doc's poetry books (Petrarch's Laura, the girl in "Black Marigolds") and Dora's practical prostitutes. Those relationships normally expected to be exploitative or repressive are mutually beneficial —the jailor and Gay; McKinley the diver and the Prohibition agents *and* the bootlegger; a landowner and trespassing bums; the police and a riotous party; even the whorehouse and the Ladies' Anti-Vice League. This rich variety of viable relationships is possible because all elements of the community share a quality that is most explicit in Steinbeck's description of Mack and the boys. He calls them "the Beauties, the Virtues, the Graces" because in a world of greed and rapacity—"ruled by tigers with ulcers, rutted by strictured bulls, scavenged by blind jackals," they "avoid the trap" of ambition. To this imagery of maimed animals is opposed a version of the Peaceable Kingdom, in which Mack and the boys "dine delicately with the tigers, fondle the frantic heifers, and wrap up the crumbs to feed the seagulls of Cannery Row." Their lack of material gain is not seen as lack of ability. Doc is certain that these "bums" can "get money." But "they just know the nature of things too well to be caught in that wanting." To Hazel's observation that Mack could have been President of the United States had he wanted to be, Jones replies, "What could he do with it if he had it?"

The novel's informing spirit is the *Tao Teh Ching* of Lao-Tze, a Chinese philosopher of the sixth century B.C. Like *Cannery Row*, the *Tao Teh Ching* was written in a time of brutal war ("Period of the Fighting States") and, in reaction to those conditions, presented a system of human values devoid of all those qualities that had brought on that war. It is interesting in this connection to quote from the prefatory remarks of two well-known editions of the *Tao* published just before *Cannery Row:*

For Laotze's book . . . teaches the wisdom of appearing foolish, the success of appearing to fail, the strength of weakness . . . if I were asked what antidote could be found . . . to cure this contentious modern world of its inveterate belief in force and struggle for power, I would name this book. . . . [Lao-Tze] has the knack of

making Hitler and other dreamers of world mastery appear foolish
and ridiculous.

—LIN YUTANG, *The Wisdom of China and India* (1942)

And the Western world might well temper its characteristic faults
by taking Laotzu to heart. . . . "Laotzu is one of our chief weapons
against tanks, artillery and bombs."

—WITTER BYNNER, *The Way of Life* (1944)

That Steinbeck was familiar with Lao-Tze's little text of
forty or so pages is certain, and most probably he was familiar
with it in the Lin Yutang translation, although several others
were also available. In *Journal of a Novel* (1951) he listed
Lao-Tze along with Plato, Christ, and Buddha as "the great
ones." Significantly, Ed Ricketts, to whom *Cannery Row* is
dedicated, was much attracted to Taoism and refers to it several times in his letters and unpublished papers. In chapter two
Steinbeck speculates that Lee Chong, who takes up most of the
first chapter and with whose name (which is similar to that of
Lao-Tze's famous disciple Chuangtse) that chapter begins, is
"more than a Chinese grocer. He must be. Perhaps he is evil
balanced and held suspended by good—an Asian planet held
to its orbit by the pull of Lao-Tze and held away from Lao-Tze
by the centrifugality of abacus and cash register. . . ." Doc
himself sometimes reads aloud to Lee Chong in English from
the poetry of Li Po, a figure associated with Taoism. In this
context, even the novel's ancient and mysterious Chinaman is
suggestive.

Taoism rejects the desire for material goods, fame, power, and even the holding of fixed or strong opinions—all of which lead to violence. Instead, man is to cultivate simple physical enjoyments and the inner life. To be obscure is to be wise; to fail is to succeed; in human relationships force always defeats itself; even laws are a form of violence; the moral life is one of inaction.

These principles are generally visible throughout *Cannery Row;* frequently the consequences of their absence are illustrated in the "little inner chapters." In addition, however, much of the novel seems to exemplify specific passages in the *Tao.* Sometimes there is even a similarity of expression. Steinbeck writes in chapter two: "The word is a symbol and a delight which sucks up men and scenes, trees, plants, factories, and Pekinese. Then the Thing becomes the Word and back to Thing again, but warped and woven into a fantastic pattern. The World sucks up Cannery Row, digests it and spews it out, and the Row has taken the shimmer of the green world and the sky-reflecting seas." Surely Steinbeck's meditation upon his own creative act is reminiscent of the Gospel according to Saint John, but its similarity to the very first passage of the *Tao Teh Ching* is even more striking:

> Existence is beyond the power of words
> To define:
> Terms may be used
> But are none of them absolute.

In the beginning of heaven and earth there were no words,
Words came out of the womb of matter;
And whether a man dispassionately
Sees to the core of life
Or passionately
Sees the surface,
The core and the surface
Are essentially the same,
Words making them seem different
Only to express appearance.
If name be needed, wonder names them both:
From wonder into wonder
Existence opens.

          —WITTER BYNNER, *The Way of Life*

There are other correspondences of statement between the two works. Steinbeck's "Virtues and Graces" live with "no money, no ambitions beyond food, drink and contentment" whereas most men "in their search for contentment destroy themselves and fall wearily short of their target." Lao-Tze says, "There is no greater curse than lack of contentment./No greater sin than the desire for possession./Therefore he who is contented with contentment shall always be content" (Lin Yutang, XLVI). Steinbeck's "another peephole," through which Mack and the boys are seen in different perspective, may be a version of "Who understands Tao seems dull of comprehension;/who is advanced in Tao seems to slip backward;/ . . . Great character appears like insufficient;/Solid character appears like infirm" (Lin Yutang, XLI). When Mack and the boys will not even turn their heads to look at the Fourth of July parade because "they know what will be in the parade," they illustrate the Taoist principle that "Without stepping outside one's doors,/One can know what is happening in the world" (Lin Yutang, XLVII).

Doc himself clearly embodies the traits of a Taoist sage. He is free of all ambition. He is a consummate "wordless teacher" to the entire community. In listening seriously to Mack's schemes or to Henri's illusions, he illustrates the Taoist principle that by not believing people you turn them into liars. His involvement in the welfare of Cannery Row demonstrates that "the Sage is good at helping men"; his care and kindness toward Frankie shows that for the sage "there is no rejected (useless) person" (Lin Yutang, XXVII). In his study of a tide pool or even a stinkbug, he conforms to the Taoist precept that one should look to Nature to know oneself, one's real human nature. "He didn't need a clock. . . . He could feel a tide change in his sleep." He is at one with his total environment—including the whorehouse, Lee Chong's, the Palace Flophouse—and thus in communion with the harmonious balance of Tao. At the height of his birthday party, Doc is seated calmly on a table, cross-legged in the Oriental posture of meditation. "The Sage dwells in the world peacefully, harmoniously./The people of the world are brought into a community of heart/and the Sage regards them all as his own children" (Lin Yutang, XLIX).

The world into which *Cannery Row* escapes is not a perfect one; not everyone lives according to the *Tao.* There is a series of misfortunes on Cannery Row, caused seemingly by some vague natural force about which "there is no explaining." But there is little in *Cannery Row* of the kind of evil men bring upon themselves through "greed, acquisitiveness, meanness, egotism and self-interest"; or through the desire to impose one's own standards on others; or even a single standard on oneself. And these incidents serve as contrasts to the book's theme. The poet Wallace Stevens could have been quoting Lao-Tze in his well-known line, "A violent order is disorder"; and his corollary statement, "A great disorder is an order," could be the epigraph for *Cannery Row.* For Steinbeck's created world is characterized by its rich variety, its benevolent chaos: "Cannery Row is a poem, a stink, a grating noise, a quality of light, a tone, a habit, a nostalgia, a dream. . . . tin and iron and rust and splintered wood, chipped pavement and weedy lots and junk heaps, sardine canneries. . . ." The same rich variety is evident in all its parts: Lee Chong's grocery store, with its hodge-podge of every conceivable commodity ("but one," Dora's), in and out of season; the Carmel River, which, though short, has a long and varied list of characteristics— "everything a river should have"; Doc's lab, with its scientific apparatus, double bed, phonograph, cookstove, poetry books, and lady visitors; Eddie's "wining" jugs, containing bourbon, wine, scotch, beer, and even grenadine mixed together; the great tide pool (a microcosm of "the cosmic Monterey") in which Doc collects his specimens and in which is found such a variety of life forms and modes of survival. All are patterns of the rich community of Cannery Row and of the novel itself —both its form and content.

In this light, Steinbeck's prefatory analogy of letting the stories ooze into the book by themselves, like delicate sea worms into a collecting jar, rather than forcing them into an order, becomes also a moral statement. (There is no formal order in the *Tao Teh Ching*, either.) Mack learns that the first party failed because "we forced her," and that the second will succeed if they just "let it happen." Steinbeck tells us that those celebrations that are "controlled and dominated" are "not parties at all but acts and demonstrations, about as spontaneous as peristalsis and as interesting as its end product." William, the first bouncer at Dora's Bear Flag Restaurant, commits suicide because, unlike Alfred, his successor, he tries to force himself on people and is rejected. Henri can love boats and be happy because he does not drive himself to the logical conclusion of finishing his boat and thus having to go out upon the water, which he fears. On the other hand, Mrs. Malloy is unhappy because she wants to do such things as "force" lace curtains upon the windowless boiler in which she lives. The ambitious wife of the landowner in the hilarious frog-hunting episode fails as a wife because she forces her compulsive neatness upon her husband. The hitchhiker is ejected from the car because he expects everyone to hold the same principles about drinking that he does. Doc knows he is a "free man" because he can indulge the rich variety of his inclinations without fear of contradictions—Bach and Debussy, *Faust* and "Black Marigolds"; even, and at the same time, Palestrina masses and sexual intercourse. In fact, he himself looks "half Christ, half satyr."

The twin themes of *Cannery Row,* then, around which the novel's characters and events casually but effectively arrange themselves, are the escape from Western material values—the necessity to "succeed" in the world; and the escape from Western activism—the necessity to impose order or direction. Like Lao-Tze, Steinbeck elaborates these two escapes into a system of "Virtues and Graces."

THE PEARL

The second piece of fiction (completed in February 1945) that Steinbeck wrote after returning from his overseas assignment continues his exploration of the capitalist ethic. Whereas *Cannery Row* presents an invented, surrogate world in which that ethic has already been rejected, the new work considers the conditions and process of the rejection itself. It differs from *Cannery Row* also in its tight structure—parallel planes of meaning moving together with the inevitability of fate; and in its prose style, which is poetic yet as objective and realistic as a camera. Many of the book's important moments (such as the "visions" Kino sees in the surface of the pearl) and even interchanges between the characters (Kino and the pearl buyers,

Kino and his wife Juana at the end) are accomplished in almost purely visual terms. This cinematic quality is further enhanced by Steinbeck's approximation of a film score, his attempt to portray various emotional states of his protagonist through the description of musical themes, or leitmotivs, especially those identified with the family, the pearl, and evil. These accompany the action and help convey its meaning through their occurrence, their changing tempo and orchestration, their displacement of one another, their blending together, conflict, or even absence. Just as *Of Mice and Men* was consciously written like a play to be read, so *The Pearl* approaches a cinematic experience in reading.

Steinbeck found the basic material for his novelette in an incident he had heard about in Mexico five years earlier and had told in some two hundred words in *Sea of Cortez* (1941). An Indian boy in La Paz, Mexico (Baja California), finds a great pearl but cannot sell it for its true value because of the organized efforts of the crooked pearl buyers. After many difficulties and much suffering, realizing he cannot beat them, he throws his treasure back into the sea rather than sell it for less than its true value or suffer the further consequences of opposing the pearl buyers. In its retelling, this anecdote is considerably elaborated and some crucial changes are made. The Indian boy who found "an unbelievable pearl" desired only to "never work again. . . . be drunk as long as he wished," and subscribe enough Masses in his village church to atone for his sins and "pop him out of purgatory like a squeezed watermelon seed."

Kino, an Indian pearl diver, wants the money to improve his material and social position—to have a proper marriage in the church, better clothes, a rifle and, most important, an education for his small son, who "will read and open the books . . . will know writing. . . . will make numbers, and these things will make us free because he will know . . . and through him we will know."

Although *The Pearl* lacks any of the more precise parallels to Lao-Tze found in *Cannery Row,* it could hardly illustrate more fully that philosopher's central precept: "No lure is greater than to possess what others want, no disaster greater than not to be content with what one has, no presage of evil greater than that man should be wanting to get more." Before Kino's final rejection of these desires, he is attacked and wounded three times; beats and kicks his wife, Juana; has his house burned to the ground and his canoe, the source of his livelihood, broken; kills four men; together with his family is hunted like an animal and his son killed. Only then, like the Indian boy of the original story, does he throw the pearl back into the sea, thus returning himself to his previous, uncompetitive position in the social and economic system. For he sees that to improve his standard of living it is necessary to join the "circling of wolves" and "hovering of vultures" which characterize the pearl buyers who are cheating him. When the greedy Spanish doctor is first asked to treat Kino's son, Coyotito, who is suffering from a scorpion bite, he refuses. Once he hears of the pearl, he insists on making a house call to the Indian ghetto and blotted out others hung over the whole Gulf so that all sights were unreal and vision could not be trusted; so that sea and land had the sharp clarities and the vagueness of a dream."

The story's major level of reference is clearly suggested by Kino's summary of the priest's sermon, given once a year, about those Indians who tried to avoid the apparent injustices of the local pearl buyers by taking their pearls directly to the capital, but disappeared and never returned: "The loss of the pearl was a punishment visited on those who tried to leave their station. And the Father made it clear that each man and woman is like a soldier sent by God to guard some part of the castle of the Universe. And some are in the ramparts and some far deep in the darkness of the walls. But each one must remain faithful to his post and must not go running about, else the castle is in danger from the assaults of Hell." Clearly, Kino is unfaithful to his "post" and goes "running about" to seek a better one. As his brother tells him, "You have defied not the pearl buyers, but the whole structure, the whole way of life. . . ." The assigned post to which Kino awakens in the "near dark" is defined by an implicit analogy to animal life: "The roosters had been crowing for some time, and the early pigs were already beginning their ceaseless turning of twigs and bits of wood to see whether anything to eat had been overlooked. Outside the brush house in the tuna clump, a little covey of birds chittered and flurried their wings." That is the complete opening paragraph. The trapped ant and the moth seeking its flame (discussed above) follow immediately upon Kino's rising from his sleeping mat.

This animal imagery is reinforced by the often repeated contrast (sometimes in the same sentence) between the town —in which dwell the Spanish-Mexican doctor, the priest, and the pearl buyers—and Kino's proper "post," the outlying barrio where he lives with his people. The latter live in small brush houses with dirt floors and doorless doorways; the townspeople live in large stone and plaster houses guarded by solid gates. For breakfast, Kino has tortilla and pulque, from an earthen jug, squatting in the dirt; the doctor has sweet biscuits and chocolate, out of a silver pot, served in bed. And there are other ways in which the essential and fixed differences between the two "posts" in this "castle of the Universe" are insisted upon.

In contrast to this kind of difference, however, Steinbeck presents another equally relevant to his theme. In their closed-up, dark, stone and plaster houses the townsmen hear only the drip of artificial fountains and the singing of caged birds; the brush houses of the barrio, open to the larger natural world, "leaked light and air," and the Indians listen to the lapping of waves on the beach and coveys of birds in the bushes. Steinbeck's selection of these details is too patterned to be accidental. In his stone and plaster house, the doctor awakens alone, bored and frustrated. Kino awakens to his natural world and to his family, and it is always "perfect among mornings"; "It was very good." He feels deeply that "this is safety, this is warmth, this is the Whole." This feelings of security and belonging which he shares with the other Indians is manifested also in "the gift he had from his people," a Jungian racial memory through which he shares not only their past history but beyond her husband's "I am a man." It means to her that he will spend his strength in hopeless struggle against immovable mountains and seas which would destroy him, "and yet it was this thing that made him a man." Both the challenge and the defeat are "right." Perhaps this is a version of our tragic human condition.

For Kino, that tragedy will become real when he finds the huge pearl, which in its very existence through "an accident . . . a grain of sand," seems an exception to this normal, stable, ordered world. Even the oyster in which the accidental huge pearl is found is exceptional, "lying by itself, not covered with its clinging brothers" like the others. Kino, too, will go his own way, "and his face grew crafty." He moves from his earlier feelings of "safety" and "warmth" into "a cold and lonely outside. He felt alone and unprotected. . . ." Asked whom he fears, he replies, "Everyone"; his voice becomes "hard and cold" and a "brooding hate" grows in him. (This progression is beautifully signaled in his three encounters with the dog.) From this point until his fight at the mountain pool, Kino is described increasingly in animal terms. "He was an animal now, for hiding, for attacking, and he lived only to preserve himself and his family." He hisses at his wife "like a snake," sleeps where a deer had slept, has "an animal light in his eyes," and runs "for the high place as nearly all animals do when pursued," instinctively employing all the ruses of a fox. Before ambushing his pursuers, he takes off all his clothes, edges down the rocks "like a slow lizard," and with the soft gentle "Song of the Family" in his heart having turned "fierce and sharp and feline as the snarl of a puma," he leaps with deadly effect upon his three pursuers.

All the elements of an adventurous success story are present: the ambition to rise above one's circumstances, the courage and skill to overcome unscrupulous enemies and overwhelming obstacles, even violent and successful mortal struggles against heavy odds. The death of Coyotito, their son, by a stray bullet would seem to call for a tearful scene at the grave, after which Kino and Juana, somewhat sadly but resolutely, resume their journey to a presumably better future, which he will ensure by continuing to exercise those qualities that have lifted him from his previous condition. *The Pearl,* however, is not a conventional success story in these terms. The "success" in the story lies in Kino's rejection of this way of life, his refusal to buy advancement in life at that price, his return to his assigned post, not in the "castle" of the priest's medieval Christian metaphor but in the order of Nature. He has learned what Juana knew with her female instinct: "This pearl is evil. Let us destroy it before it destroys us." So they return to the town not in single file with Juana behind, as they had left, but side by side, Juana carrying their dead son, Kino the useless rifle. And when they reach the sea, Kino offers the pearl to Juana for her to throw back into the water from which it came. That she surrenders this decisive action to her husband is profoundly meaningful. On this level, the ending represents not defeat but victory, pyrrhic though it may be. After all, they have rejected only "The Pearl of the *World*" (italics added), as it is called several times and as the story was named in its first publication.

Although Steinbeck was correct in calling his first 200-word version of his story a "parable," that term is not quite accurate for *The Pearl.* Not only is it too long for a parable, but too complex and rich in meaning. "Allegory" is a better term, especially if we have in mind its rich medieval forms, for this novelette exists on a number of levels. It is also an allegory of the soul. The title itself indicates several possible sources. First to come to mind is Matthew 13:45, 46, Jesus' parable of the "pearl of great price." But, as we have seen before, Steinbeck's reading led him much further afield than his Bible. There is also the anonymous medieval poem, *Pearl*, and, somewhat more recondite, the gnostic fragment called "Acts of Thomas," which contains one passage sometimes printed separately as "The Song of the Pearl." In all three of these sources the pearl is read as a symbol for the soul, and the allegory is understood to treat of its redemption. In fact, the gnostic passage is called also "The Hymn of the Soul." There are suggestions that Steinbeck had all three sources in mind. From the medieval poem Steinbeck may have taken the idea for the music images and, most important, the father-child-pearl association. In the "Acts of Thomas" he could have found the idea of the soul's being in bondage and the perilous quest of redeeming it. However, Steinbeck's allegory of the pearl-soul goes far beyond all of these sources.

Although almost all the action is Kino's and it is he who says

several times, "This pearl has become my soul," and "If I give
it up I shall lose my soul," nevertheless it is *his* soul in an
interestingly indirect manner. Kino finds the pearl after Juana
has prayed that he may find a pearl to pay a doctor to cure their
little son of a scorpion sting. There is never any question but
that the pearl is for the child, even after the doctor is not
needed. In the boat, while Kino is hesitating to open the
unusual oyster, Juana "put her hand on Coyotito's covered
head. 'Open it,' she said softly." When the oyster is opened
and the pearl disclosed, immediately, for no apparent reason,
"Instinctively Juana went to Coyotito where he lay in his
father's blanket. She lifted the poultice of seaweed and looked
. . . the swelling was going out of the baby's shoulder, the
poison was receding from its body." Later, when Juana steals
the pearl from Kino's hiding place to throw it away, fearful of
the danger it has brought, she pauses first at Coyotito's crib.
Near the end of the book, when Kino urges his wife to keep
Coyotito quiet so that he may surprise and kill their pursuers,
who would take away the pearl, Juana replies, "He will not cry.
. . . He knows." Furthermore, the very name Coyotito ("little
coyote") signifies the animal nature of a creature which does
not have a soul; his crying is once described as like "a coyote
pup."

The redeeming of the pearl, then, is equivalent to raising
this being from an animal to a human state. For clearly the
pearl symbolizes not the usual religious definition of "soul," but
human consciousness and potential, those qualities that cause

man to separate himself from the rest of Nature. This is sig-
nified by the education which the pearl will buy, to literally
raise Coyotito from the almost animal existence into which he
was born. Kino's identification of the pearl with his own soul
is by two extensions. First, Coyotito is his son—himself a child
again, an extension of himself into the future. Secondly,
Coyotito's education (what the pearl will buy and thus its
equivalent), or soul, "will make us free . . . he will know and
through him we will know." In this extension, the allegory of
the soul now applies not only to Kino but to the entire Indian
community. Consider also that Kino, as the priest reminds
him, is named after the Jesuit missionary Father Eusebius
Kino, a great saver of souls among the Indians of that region.

In any allegory about the soul, there are evil powers that
attempt to thwart its redemption. In Steinbeck's novelette
these are conspicuously mysterious, referred to as "the dark
unhuman things," "watchful evil," "dark creeping things,"
"shadowy and dreadful," "the dark ones," and the like. They
are the ones who three times attack Kino to rob him of the
pearl. The two trackers and the horseman, also, who pursue
Kino and his family are made symbolically suggestive. But
again on this level of the allegory, the moral is in the ending.
For neither is Kino defeated by these evil powers, nor does he
redeem his pearl. Instead, he chooses to renounce it after
overcoming the powers of darkness. Kino refuses the option of
attaining his soul (a distinct identity) at such continued cost,
preferring to *undefine* himself, returning the seed of individual

soul to Whitman's cosmic "Float," Emerson's (and Casy's) Oversoul, thus going back to the blameless bosom of Nature in a quasi-animal existence—"in the near dark" of the story's opening sentence.

It is also possible to see in *The Pearl* still another of Steinbeck's several Eden myths, with a unique twist. After eating of the forbidden tree ("Yes, God punished Kino because he rebelled against the way things are"), after being expelled from the Garden ("We must go away"), and after experiencing the land that lies "east of Eden" (the rock and desert landscape of their flight), Kino and Juana *return* to Eden, put the apple back on the tree, as it were. They reject the "fortunate fall" which would give man the burden of an immortal soul to save or damn, and return to an animal-like life, Adam and Eve before the Fall. All these readings are suggested within the structure and rich texture of *The Pearl.*

The allegory extends also into Mexican Indian mythology. Although Steinbeck always presents Kino and Juana as basically Indian in consciousness, he carefully leaves their particular origins vague, because the peoples of Baja California seem to have been much weaker in religious ritualism than those of the mainland and almost nothing is known of the ancient religion of the Seri Indians of the La Paz area except that they existed on an animistic level which attributed life and supernatural powers to all things. (Coyotito, however, is named after one of the four Seri clans—Coyote.) Therefore, Steinbeck uses mythical elements from various Indian cultures, but especially the Mayan and the Aztec, which are dominant in our general knowledge of pre-Columbian Mexico. This material is so rich, and Steinbeck's utilization of it so detailed that it bulks larger than the Christian elements in the novelette as well as in the consciousness of Kino and Juana themselves.

To begin with, in stressing so often the novelette's imprecise landscape, its "mist," its "hazy mirage . . . the uncertain air . . . so that all sights were unreal and vision could not be trusted," Steinbeck suggests not only the generally dreamlike settings of fabular literature, but quite specifically a Mayan belief that in the most recent creation the gods saw that they had made man too gifted and therefore had to place a mist before his eyes so that the secrets of the universe would not be revealed to him. Another general and significant aspect is the novelette's time span. In the incredibly accurate Mayan calendar, at the end of one of the major cycles (fifty-two years), and before the beginning of the next, there were the *Uayeb*, "five unlucky days" of great significance, including ritualistic destruction of furniture, bloodletting, lamentation and extinguishing of all fires—at the end of which a new fire was kindled and a new cycle began. During these five days, possible catastrophe was imminent, and it was best to stay at home. It can hardly be coincidental that from the morning of the day on which Kino wakens at the beginning of the novel, and during which he finds the pearl, to sunset on the evening of the story's ending, when Kino and Juana return from their journey and throw the pearl back into the sea, the time span is exactly five days, at the end of which destruction and suffering, man and wife resume their usual cycle.

Another large symbolic element is the novelette's constant and suggestive use of light and darkness. Generally among these Indians (as other peoples) darkness is feared because it is then that evil forces and the creatures of darkness are free to bring about man's destruction. In *The Pearl* this association is suggested throughout and often insisted upon: "and with the darkness came the music of evil again," "his fear of dark and the devils that haunt the night." The Indians cover their faces against the darkness; the three assaults upon Kino are in the night and, as discussed above, the assailants linked with the world of darkness. In various ways, even the doctor, the priest (both of whom visit Kino at night), and the pearl buyers are linked to darkness. Thus the scene in which Kino begins to fear the light and associate himself with the darkness, after killing one assailant and finding his house on fire, is significant. His flight begins in darkness; he attacks his three pursuers at night; and it is then that his son is killed. The owl, one of the Mayan symbols of evil and death, is conspicuous in the night scenes.

Inevitably associated with night is the moon, in Mayan mythology one of the two important sky gods, inconstant and malicious in character. In the novelette the moon reappears from behind the clouds to show Juana the pearl after Kino loses it; as the clouds again cover the moon, she thinks of completing her intention of throwing the pearl into the sea, but the moon again reappears and shows her the two men lying in the path ahead of her, one of whom is Kino, whom she runs to help. The moon also reappears, rising sooner than expected, as Kino is preparing to leap upon his pursuers, causing the delay (and perhaps Coyotito's cry) which allows the fatal shot. The pearl itself is described "perfect as the moon," is seen to glitter in moonlight, and reflects the moon in its surface, thus reinforcing frequent suggestions that the pearl is evil. As in Mayan mythology the sun is the other important sky god, associated with the powers of life and goodness and antagonist to the moon, so in the novelette daylight dispels the powers of darkness, a process that is generally suggested in *The Pearl* by Steinbeck's descriptions of the dawn. In reference to this struggle and the pearl's association with the moon, it is relevant that Kino's name has its origin not only in the Jesuit missionary, but in the Mayan word *Kin,* meaning sun. The clouds which try to hide the moon in the above passages come from the south, domain of the sun. Of the several visions that Kino sees in the pearl's surface, all are delusions except one, the last, the only one seen in the open light of day, just before he flings it back into the sea: "He looked into its surface and it was gray and ulcerous. Evil faces peered from it into his eyes, and he saw the light of burning. . . . the pearl was ugly; it was gray like a malignant growth . . . the music of the pearl distorted and insane."

Steinbeck's reading in Mexican sources was extensive, and mythology had always a particular interest for him. He chose his Indian materials carefully to reinforce his other levels of meaning. In this novelette of eighty pages Steinbeck attains what is very difficult and rare in even the best allegories—a congruence of all its referential levels. *The Pearl* achieves a dimension beyond that possible to realistic fiction.

THE WAYWARD BUS

Almost as if to demonstrate his mastery and virtuosity in the fabular forms of literature, a little more than a year after completing *The Pearl,* Steinbeck wrote a novel almost four times as long in which his own criteria for the qualities of "parable" are conspicuously lacking. *The Wayward Bus* does not at all have a "set-aside and raised-up feeling," an aesthetic distance from the reader; nor has it the simplification into "only good and bad things and black and white things . . . and no in-between anywhere." Rather, more than any of his previous novels, it is almost embarrassingly direct and intimate in both language and detail, its characters and themes realistically ambiguous. Also contributing to this lack of the immediate suggestiveness associated with parables and allegories is the large amount of purely realistic detail. Unlike *The Pearl,* there is not always "significance" in the minute descriptions of setting, characters, and incidents.

The novel's fabular intentions are, however, clearly set forth in its epigraph, taken from the prologue of a fifteenth-century morality play (spelling modernized):

I pray you all give audience,
And hear this matter with reverence,
By figure a moral play:
The *Summoning of Everyman* called it is,
That of our lives and ending shows
How transitory we be all [every] day.

The play itself is an allegory in which the main character, Everyman, is summoned by Death to appear before God and give an account of his life, on which he will be judged. One by one, all his good qualities, presented as personifications, forsake him—Strength, Beauty, Knowledge, Kindred, Discretion, and so forth. Only Good Deeds will stand by him and speak for him at God's throne. Quite probably without its epigraph the novel's basic structure would go unnoticed, for here as elsewhere in his fiction Steinbeck's use of archetypal sources is creative, not imitative. Neither the cast of personifications nor the obvious circumstances of the "moral play" are repeated in his novel. Rather, Everyman is represented by several characters, and his journey to the grave becomes a shuttle-bus connection between two stations on different highways.

There are ten major characters in the novel, each introduced and described as directly as in a play. Seven of them become passengers on the wayward bus, driven by Juan Chicoy and his helper, Pimples. Alice Chicoy, the driver's wife, stays behind at the lunchroom bus station. In terms of their personal qualities they fall into two major groups. Juan Chicoy, Camille Oaks, and Ernest Horton, although differing widely in many respects, share four attributes: honest knowledge of themselves, an objective view of their relationship to the world, distinct ability in their professions, and sexual attractiveness. These three are further distinguished by bearing scars on their bodies, physical evidence of their real encounters with the world. Juan has scars on his face and is missing part of one finger; Camille has deep forceps marks on her temples from a difficult birth; Ernest Horton's scars are implied by his Congressional Medal of Honor—and, ironically, considering his job as a seller of joke gadgets, his artificial crushed foot. It is interesting for later developments that these three characters share among them the stigmata (side, hands, and feet). Juan Chicoy, however, by virtue of his initials, his role as driver of the bus, and even his offer to wash the feet of others, is intended as a kind of Christ figure.

The second group consists of seven characters who are clearly inferior. Each is in some way hypocritical or weak and lacking in most or all of the first group's qualities. Their physical defects (Mildred's weak eyes, Pimples' acne) are natural, probably temporary. But each is endowed with attributes suggesting one of the seven deadly sins (Wrath, Pride, Avarice, Sloth, Envy, Gluttony, and Lust—or Luxury, to use, as Steinbeck does the archaic term). Alice Chicoy, with her almost constant ill humor, her vicious attacks upon Pimples, her hysterical outburst at Norma, and her constant (and final) anger at flies, clearly represents Wrath. The most detailed and strongest portrait in the book is of Bernice Pritchard. Her sexlessness, self-satisfaction, hypocrisy, and extreme conventionality ("having few actual perceptions, she lived by rules") express themselves in a selfish Pride which keeps her always isolated from the other passengers and scornful of them. Her husband, Elliott, is a businessman whose description is a set piece, almost literally copied from Sinclair Lewis's *Babbitt* in every detail. His conversations with Horton about business deals clearly reveal his Avarice. Van Brunt's constant criticism yet refusal to do anything, to participate in the decisions and take consequent responsibilities, marks him as Sloth. Norma's dream life centers upon Hollywood movie stars. Her desire to become one of them is so strong that her Envy causes her to live a life of illusion, wearing a wedding ring to bed, pretending she is the bride of Clark Gable. Pimples, whose horrible acne is aggravated by his constant eating of candy bars, pies, and cakes, in which he encourages others also, is Gluttony. Mildred Pritchard, Bernice's daughter, provides perhaps the least definite association. She and Pimples are linked together in various ways, being also the most sympathetic of the group. Her related role as Luxury to Pimples' Gluttony is suggested by her economic position and privileges: college, clothes, money, vacations, and her sexual indulgence.

In the original morality play, Everyman is given permission to seek some companion "from this vale terrestrial . . . that way to me lead to God's judgement" and is refused by Fellowship,

Kindred, Cousin, and Goods. Good Deeds would follow him, but is weighed down by Everyman's sins and directs him to his sister "called Knowledge, which shall with you abide,/To help you to make that dreadful reckoning." Knowledge—which in this context is understood as the acknowledgement of sin, or self-knowledge—leads Everyman to Confession, who gives him a "precious jewel" called Penance, after which Everyman dons the "garment of contrition." Although only Good Deeds, now freed from bonds, can accompany Everyman into the hereafter, Beauty, Strength, Discretion, and Five Wits, under the direction of Knowledge, accompany him on his pilgrimage to the very edge of the grave.

That the passengers of *The Wayward Bus* are also on a pilgrimage is strongly suggested. They leave from Rebel Corners and their destination sounds similarly suggestive—San Juan de la Cruz (St. John of the Cross). It is spring, a traditional time for pilgrimages, as in the *Canterbury Tales;* in fact the variety and presentation of Steinbeck's characters, though more scattered, is much like Chaucer's presentation in the "Prologue." The spiritual plane of this pilgrimage is suggested by several details. The modern "high way" is imperiled by the flooding San Ysidro river, which, although named after a patron saint of agriculture, drowns livestock and washes away topsoil as well as making the bridges across it unsafe. The passengers therefore elect to leave this "high way" and return to the abandoned and difficult road of their ancestors, encountering there, painted on fences, such messages as "Repent, for the Kingdom of Heaven is at hand," "Sinner, come to God," and "It is late," ironically interspersed with other cures: "Jay's Drugs" and "Cyrus Noble—The Doctor's Whiskey." The "old, old bus" has recently been named Sweetheart, in pointed contrast to its previous name, still barely legible, *El Gran Poder de Jesus* ("the great power of Jesus"), and is hung with trifles and souvenirs, which Steinbeck calls penates—household gods. When this old battered world of a bus is abandoned in the mud by Juan Chicoy, the passengers find themselves beneath a rock cliff, on which is painted "in great faint letters, REPENT," and from which some caves "like dark eyes" stare down upon them. It is here, beneath this message, that the sinners, like Everyman, experience self-knowledge, after which Juan Chicoy returns to his helpless charges and resumes his guidance.

This self-knowledge comes to each of them through some relationship with his fellows, that relationship in turn sometimes providing for the other one of the Good Deeds that may alone speak for Everyman at his judgment. Elliott Pritchard, representing the essence of Western capitalistic society, is responsible to a large extent for the impoverished spiritual condition of the youthful Pimples and Norma. "Pimples took most of his ideas from moving pictures and the rest from the radio" and advertising clichés—"It's rich in food energy. . . . about three o'clock in the afternoon, when you get a let-down." The self-knowledge Mr. Pritchard must face, therefore, is most brutal. Horton makes him recognize that his business ethics and ideal of "service" are pure avarice, nothing more than "high-class blackmail." And Camille, a professional stripper and entertainer, provides him with the recognition that his "fatherly" interest in her welfare is but a sexual form of the same greed. Van Brunt through his repelling sick body causes Mr. Pritchard to recognize that, even while doing a good deed by attending him, "he hated this man because he was dying. He inspected his hatred in amazement. . . . 'What kind of thing am I?' "

To other passengers, self-knowledge comes somewhat more gently. Before making love to Juan on rotting straw in an old rat-infested barn, Mildred is forced to admit her self-indulgent, lustful nature: "I don't want you to think it's you. It's me. I know what I want. I don't even like you." She is even forced to make the advances. "You don't give me any pride. . . . any violence to fall back on later." Mildred, in turn, earns a good deed when through a description of her undergarments she brings to Van Brunt the embarrassing knowledge that his attentions to her are those of a nasty old man.

Although Pimples Carson wants to be called Kit, to imply qualities he wished he had, Norma forces him to recognize both his gluttonous sexual ineptness and his related repulsive acne in a painfully hilarious love scene. Later, he makes his penance by purposely immersing himself and his new clothes in mud. Norma herself comes to self-knowledge most gently and gradually as Camille, that specialist in reality and the condition of the sexes, takes her in hand. Pimples' sexual attack on her provides Norma's penance, and ironically, perhaps one of his good deeds also.

"Everyman, I will go with thee, and be thy guide./In thy

most need to go by thy side." However, this promise by Knowledge in the morality play is not extended to all the pilgrims in the wayward bus. Of the seven who exemplify one of the deadly sins, Alice (Wrath), although urged to become a passenger, refuses. She purposely chooses the oblivion of drunkenness instead. Perhaps her knowledge of her own condition is already sufficient, but she refuses the penance necessary to purge herself. Van Brunt, victim of a paralyzing stroke at the end of the novel, is the emblem of sloth itself as he lies immobile on the back seat. It is Bernice Pritchard who presents the most terrible picture. Pride is traditionally the worst of the seven deadly sins. It has been called the unforgivable sin (the sin against the Holy Ghost) because it causes the sinner to refuse the Holy Ghost and thus even the knowledge of his own sinfulness. Therefore, Bernice Pritchard, who, except for Kathy in *East of Eden*, is Steinbeck's most evil woman, quite pointedly refuses knowledge, which quite fittingly is offered to her in the guise of her husband's conjugal rape on the dirt floor of a cave. The scourging of her body, which she accomplishes by gouging her face with her nails and pouring dirt (mixed with the ash of campfires) upon herself, is not the penance it would seem, but a preparation to exercise her pride even further in the complete domination of her husband by exploiting his guilt feelings. As all the other passengers contribute good deeds to free the mired bus (except the paralyzed Van Brunt), carrying rocks, digging, and pushing, Bernice Pritchard sits inside, isolated in her pride.

Just as Juan Chicoy does not permanently abandon the bus

but returns to dig it out of the mud and set its passengers again on their pilgrimage, so Steinbeck, too, embraces the human condition and does not withhold some measure of sympathy and understanding for each of his characters, no matter how fallen, even Bernice Pritchard. Perhaps Bernice's whole personality had its beginning in the fact that she was born with "what is known as a nun's hood, which prevented her from experiencing any sexual elation from her marriage," Steinbeck writes. Her husband's avarice was perhaps caused by the birth of a sister when he was five years old and the consequent rejection, sense of unworthiness, and "cold loneliness" from which he still suffers. Similarly, Alice is still haunted by the nature of her first sexual experience with a callous and brutal person. Van Brunt remembers his father lying "a gray helpless worm in bed for eleven months" following a stroke. He himself has already suffered two of them and is waiting for the third, which may leave him as helpless as his father. Pimples and, to some extent, Mildred suffer from the real but passing pangs of physically and mentally growing up. They both have good qualities, as does Norma also, which they will be able to exercise better after maturing some. If there is any moral on this level of the novel, it is no more cheering than that given by Brett in Hemingway's *The Sun Also Rises* ("It feels good deciding not to be a bitch.") and it is given by a somewhat similar character, Camille: ". . . everybody's a tramp some time or other. Everybody. And the worst tramps of all are the ones that call it something else."

But the novel does not rest here, for the moral of *Everyman*, that salvation begins with self-knowledge, is reinforced at the end of the novel by the bus arriving within sight of its destination, which appears almost as a distant glimpse of the heavenly city: "Far ahead and a little to the left a cluster of lights came into view—little lights winking with distance, lost and lonely in the night, remote and cold and winking, strung on chains." This is San Juan de la Cruz, a fictitious town, named after the sixteenth-century Spanish mystic whose best-known work is *Dark Night of the Soul.* The resemblances which Steinbeck's novel bears to this work are more than passing; and they at all points reinforce the *Everyman* structure and morality.

The "dark night" of the title is a metaphor for the soul's condition as it struggles, in the first stage, to free itself of the seven deadly sins, the natures of which are treated in separate chapters, such as "Of certain spiritual imperfections which beginners have with respect to the habit of pride." Another chapter treats of "the second capital sin, which is avarice." As in *Everyman*, self-knowledge is of central importance in this scheme, being "the first and principal benefit caused by this . . . dark night of contemplation." It is not difficult to find descriptions of the souls in *Dark Night of the Soul* that are similar to the manifestations of sin in the characters of *The Wayward Bus.* One of the three kinds of Wrath discussed seems to fit Alice very well: ". . . they become irritated at the sins of others, and keep watch on those others with uneasy zeal." The analysis of Gluttony in terms of "sweetness" and immaturity certainly fits Pimples; and that gluttons tend to do wrong penance by abusing the body, "which is no more than the penance of beasts," also applies to him. Many such similarities can be drawn. That the whole process should utilize the journey or pilgrimage motif seems inevitable.

There is still another parallel between the characters in *The Wayward Bus* and *Dark Night of the Soul.* Just as Steinbeck sets apart Juan Chicoy, Camille Oaks, and Ernest Horton from those who are still in process of purging the seven deadly sins, so the Spanish mystic separates "proficients" from "beginners" in the stages of spiritual exercise. Like Steinbeck's corresponding characters, these "proficients" are not perfect, but simply farther along on the road to "Divine Union." For them a second "dark night" must be passed, which in *The Wayward Bus* seems to correspond to the exercises they undergo through involvement with their fellow passengers: "The afflictions and trials of the will are now very great likewise, and of such a kind that they sometimes pierce the soul with a sudden remembrance of the evils in the midst of which it finds itself, and with the uncertainty of finding a remedy for them." Surely Juan, Camille, and Horton find themselves in this second "dark night." Steinbeck's use of *Everyman* and *Dark Night of the Soul* is significant because through them he projects his understanding of the human condition in essentially traditional Christian, rather than humanistic or naturalistic, terms.

Despite this richness of structure and reference, *The Wayward Bus* does not reach the level of excellence marked by *Cannery Row* and *The Pearl.* The novel's action breaks up into simultaneous little episodes; the direct description of characters, already stereotyped, leaves little to discover; and, as suggested earlier, the extensive descriptions of setting are mostly conventional and without consequence.

In terms of Steinbeck's career, however, the novel is interesting and significant for several reasons. Through its apology for, its reasonable explanation of Elliott Pritchard and its respectful presentation of Ernest Horton, Steinbeck is backing away from the strong position taken in *Cannery Row.* There are passages in *The Wayward Bus* examining the morality of the business world that are as damning as any in the earlier novel, but Steinbeck does not seem to take the immoralities as seriously or find them as irrevocable. Another interesting aspect of the novel is its psychological, often Freudian interest in personality, per se, rather than in terms of total structure or theme. Finally, although Steinbeck consistently had used Christian symbols and imagery in his novels as *tools* of his craft, exercised upon his particular materials *(The Grapes of Wrath, In Dubious Battle),* in this latest novel the Christian themes of *Everyman* and *Dark Night of the Soul* provide the materials themselves.

These three aspects of *The Wayward Bus* suggest the major methods and preoccupations of the books which were to follow. Indeed the Christian optimism of the later books seems to be heralded by this novel's ending: "There was a little rim of lighter sky around the edge of a great dark cloud over the western mountains, and then as the cloud lifted the evening star shone out of it, clear and washed and steady."

7

✵✵✵✵✵✵✵

Burning Bright,
East of Eden,
and The Winter of Our Discontent:
ESSAYS IN CHRISTIANITY

STEINBECK's third effort in his "play-novelette" form, *Burning Bright* (following *Of Mice and Men* and *The Moon Is Down*), is without doubt the least successful book he ever published; and as a play, according to its producer, "it was dead the first night." The uncertainties of *The Wayward Bus*, published three years earlier, provided little indication of this total collapse. *Burning Bright* marks a turning point in Steinbeck's career. He was never again to achieve that fine integration of theme, material, and technique that is present to a varying but always adequate extent in his previous work. Ultimately, the reasons for this artistic collapse are bound up with profound changes in his personal life, as suggested in the discussion of *East of Eden* and in the concluding chapter of this book.

The title and epigraph of *Burning Bright* are taken from Blake's "The Tyger":

> Tyger! Tyger! burning bright,
> In the forests of the night,
> What immortal hand or eye
> Could frame thy fearful symmetry?

The poem itself, however, unlike the sources of other Steinbeck titles and epigraphs, or basic references—King Arthur and the Knights of the Round Table in *Tortilla Flat*, for example—does little to illuminate the work. From the poem's position in Blake's *Songs of Experience*, it is clearly a contrast to "The Lamb" in his earlier *Songs of Innocence*, as is stressed by the line, "Did He who made the Lamb make thee?" Perhaps Steinbeck meant to indicate no more than this awe at the variety of life, the knowledge of its terror which comes with experience, and some wonder as to the nature of a god who could create both the tiger and the lamb. On this general level it is not difficult to relate the poem to the protagonist's learning experience in the play, just as the title *Of Mice and Men* generally relates that novel to Burns's poem without providing its structural detail. But it should be kept in mind that the relevance of Steinbeck's titles and epigraphs, although frequently of central importance (*In Dubious Battle* and *The*

Wayward Bus, for example) is not always obvious. Steinbeck himself must have felt some essential connection between his book and the poem, as his working titles indicate: "Tyger! Tyger!" and "In the Forests of the Night." However, even should some more detailed and structurally essential parallel between Blake's poem and *Burning Bright* be discovered, the book's glaring faults would remain.

The story is a simple one. Joe Saul, a middle-aged man, desires a child by his young wife, Mordeen, who loves him and desires the same, but comes to believe that her husband, whose first wife had died childless three years before, is sterile. Out of love for him she chooses a young man, Victor, to make her pregnant, intending to pass off the child as her husband's and thus make him happy. Unfortunately, after the birth of the child, Joe Saul learns that he is indeed sterile and cannot understand the purity and love of his wife's gift. Victor learns it is his child and refuses to give it up, having fallen in love with Mordeen. The fourth character, Friend Ed, who is a loyal friend to both husband and wife, helps to bring about a resolution to the problem. In that resolution lies the book's moral theme. Curiously, the book is written in three "Acts," each with a different setting—"the Circus," "the Farm," "the Sea" —and its characters' occupations change accordingly, the action progressing continuously, each Act picking up where the previous one left off.

Like *The Pearl* and *The Wayward Bus,* the new work is conceived in fabular terms. The language and the three settings, Steinbeck said, are attempts to give the theme "universality of experience" and "lift the story to the parable expression of the morality play." A parable, to appropriate Robert Frost, is saying one thing in terms of another. This is very little evident in *Burning Bright*. Taking into consideration Joe Saul's first name and Mordeen's blue gown (traditional for Mary, the mother of Christ) together with the fact that the husband is not the father of the child and that the baby is born at Christmastime, the story would seem to have a level of allusion. Victor then would be the Holy Ghost or Spirit, a role supported by his lack of personal importance, his serving only to transmit the germ of life. But this level of meaning is not further extended.

As for the techniques, it is not that the progression of continuing action from circus to farm to sea is confusing or poorly accomplished; transitions are made smoothly by key bits of setting (the Christmas tree) or references in dialogue or even a farm radio blaring circus music. But this progression is totally unnecessary and superficial—a clever gadget. The special "kind of universal language" which Steinbeck devised for the book is undoubtedly its worst fault. It is studded with such synthetic gems as "friend-right," "wife-loss," and "beauty thing," and demonstrates such an insensitivity to its own implications that many serious lines had to be cut from the stage production because they caused great hilarity in the audience. The most consistent mark of Steinbeck's genius is his command of language, his ability to create different prose styles to embody materials as diverse as *Tortilla Flat* and *In Dubious Battle*. The failure of language in *Burning Bright*, in fact its return to the style of "poetic diction" used in his first two novels, from which whole sentences seem paraphrased, is surely ominous.

In the foreword Steinbeck gives a rationale for the form of *Burning Bright* which repeats his simple explanation for *Of Mice and Men* but develops much more fully the theatrical possibilities of the piece. Certainly one immediate cause for Steinbeck's failure is this stressing of theatrical over fictional qualities; *Burning Bright* looks over its shoulder at the stage so often that it falls flat as fiction. In fact, unlike its predecessors, it appeared (and failed) on the stage before it was published as a book. Similarly the narration sometimes seems crudely fictionalized stage direction (e.g., the opening paragraphs of each act) and at other times is so purely fictionalized as to render it unstageable, such as the rhapsody on Mordeen's foetus. Ironically, despite his close concern for its theatrical qualities, the production of *Burning Bright* required more extensive changes in dialogue and action than had its two predecessors. Perhaps the play-novelette form is more congenial to the conventions of a realistic stage than to expressionistic techniques, such as the telescoped passage of time (about eight months) in the second act, or the appearance of an unidentified "he" in the last part, who becomes Joe Saul, and who floods the hospital room with light by taking off his surgical mask!

Insofar as it can be separated from its expression, the major theme of *Burning Bright* is an impressive one, and worthy of a major writer—"That every man is father to all children and every child must have all men as father." Before Joe Saul learns this, he must "walk into the black" of personal crisis, where he loses his false values—the importance he attaches to personal heredity and thus to himself as a unique individual. Frequently he laments having no children: "But a man can't die this way. . . . can't scrap his blood line, can't snip the thread of his immortality"; "the line, a preciousness carried and shielded through the stormy millennia, is snapped"; "the blood stream, the pattern of me . . . like a shining filament of spider silk hanging down from the incredible ages." In each act, Joe Saul asserts his lineage back to the dawn of man, once even as far as "nature spirits." Out of this self-pride, he rejects those like Victor, who, although admittedly as good as and perhaps better than Cousin Will on the trapeze (or tractor or bridge of a ship), "has no ancestry in it." In proclaiming that "his blood is not my blood," Joe Saul reaches the height of tragic hubris. He is restored to wholeness again by learning that in fact he himself is sterile, that his wife is pregnant by another, and that the man is none other than Victor. Only then, and after understanding Mordeen's unselfish, loving motive in wanting to give him a child, can he progress in the last scene to a statement of the book's moral, and from "the child" to "our child" to "I love my son." *Burning Bright* is Steinbeck's most personalized and intimate statement of the theme of species consciousness or human solidarity that on a social level reaches its peak in *The Grapes of Wrath.*

Unfortunately, this noble tragic theme is vitiated by poor writing and by an unacceptable solution to the problem of Victor, whom Mordeen rejects as a person, merely *using* him, as a stud. He is given a crunching blow on the head and dumped into the harbor when he insists upon recognition as the father of Mordeen's child. "There are many Victors," says Friend Ed after his deed; "there will always be a Victor." Even worse, although Victor is initially portrayed as combining the selfish thinking of Alice Chicoy ("the self-centered chaos of childhood") and the pool-hall morality of Louie, the other bus driver in *The Wayward Bus*, ("A jump in the hay is a jump in the hay"), by the end of the novelette he is in many ways an admirable character. He really tries to go away and forget his part in the Saul family. He has even come to understand that "a jump in the hay" is not the height of human sexuality. He speaks the most moving poetry in the novel (Act Two), and all of this occurs through the power of his one experience with Mordeen, whom he has come to love. It is this changed Victor who is murdered, in a story illustrating that "every child must have all men as father." The stage production was sensible enough to mitigate Victor's fate by having him shanghaied on a long voyage.

The novelette ends with the reaffirmation, "It is the race, the species that must go staggering on"; that despite our human insanities and evil, our "flickering intelligence," some-where "there is a shining." The source of that shining was to be explored in his next published novel, already under way.

EAST OF EDEN

The first work in Steinbeck's new phase offered a variation on the virgin birth (Joseph, Mary's husband, not being the father of Christ) to propose, though briefly and ineffectively, the liberal Christian message that "every child must have all men as fathers." *East of Eden* exhausts the Cain and Abel story to propose at great length, but no more effectively, the Christian message that each man is capable of choosing between good and evil.

That this message was not a part of Steinbeck's thinking when he started work on the novel five years before its publication is further proof of his new direction. Originally, his intention was to set down in story form for his two small sons (then six and four years old) an account of his ancestors, beginning with their moving from New England to the Salinas Valley in California shortly after the Civil War. Beginning his first draft, in late January 1951, after four years of false starts and confusion, he wrote, "In a sense it will be two books—the story of my county and the story of me." And although later in the same note he seems to refer to the Cain and Abel theme when he states he will tell "perhaps the greatest story of all—the story of good and evil," this first draft is titled "The Salinas Valley," and begins, "Dear Tom and John: You are little boys now, when I am writing this." His plan, later abandoned, was to have the chapters about the maternal side of his family, the Hamiltons, alternate regularly with those chapters about another family, the Trasks, who carry the Cain and Abel story. It was not until four months later, halfway through the book, that he began to consider another title—"Cain Sign"—indicating a shift in emphasis. Except for these changes, however, Steinbeck had the book's basic structure and content very well in mind.

Other revisions, of course, were made in a second draft—altering the chapter divisions and removing all those portions that were addressed to his sons and were to have prefaced each of the Hamilton chapters. These revisions, however, could not solve the problem of the novel's widely disparate materials.

The sixteen verses from Genesis that provide the novel's main theme and its title—"And Cain went out from the presence of the Lord, and dwelt in the land of Nod, on the east of Eden"—are elaborated through three generations covering fifty-six years, and the six-hundred-page novel is divided into four parts. In the first of these, Cyrus Trask fathers upon an unnamed wife a son, Adam, in 1862, who is joined by a half-brother, Charles, after Cyrus marries his second wife. The assault of Cain on Abel in this generation is represented by two vicious beatings, one almost fatal, administered by Charles, who is jealous of their father's preference for Adam. As in the Bible, this rejection is expressed in the preference of one brother's gift over that of the other. Meanwhile, in other chapters, another Cain figure is developed, Cathy, and Part One ends in the year 1900 with her marriage to Adam and, on their wedding night, her adultery with Charles. In Part Two,

Adam leaves his New England farm, coming west to the Salinas Valley with his wife, who, nine months after their wedding night, bears him nonidentical twin boys and soon afterward deserts Adam, establishing herself in Salinas as a prostitute and madam called Kate. The naming of the boys—Caleb and Aron —ends this part in the year 1902. Between this date and Part Three, nine years elapse, and this third part, although as long as Part Two, contains nothing of significance about the Trasks. In this part, we become acquainted with the Hamiltons: Samuel, Liza, and their eight children, especially Tom, Dessie, and Olive, Steinbeck's mother. Some of these portraits and events are interesting, and according to Steinbeck, all are true. In Part Four, 1912–1918, the central story is again enacted between Caleb and Aron. Their father, Adam, rejects the gift of Caleb, whose vengeance then causes the enlistment and death of Aron in World War I. The novel concludes with the suggestion that the theme will continue through Caleb and his future wife, Abra, his brother's former sweetheart. But the two bodies of material in no way influence or effectively complement each other. There are only seven brief contacts between the two families in twenty-six years. Only three of these have any significance whatsoever: Hamilton's role as midwife to Cathy; his return a year later to name the sons; his return ten years later to say farewell. There is nothing in the Hamilton chapters to reflect substantially upon the Cain and Abel story.

East of Eden's long period of gestation and gradual change in emphasis surely accounts for some of its sprawling, omnivorous nature. The major causes, however, are recorded in the epistolary journal Steinbeck kept for his friend and editor Pascal Covici during the novel's composition (one "letter" for each working day), published posthumously as *Journal of a Novel* (1969). But these causes are most meaningfully examined after some familiarity with the novel itself.

It was not Steinbeck's method *(Tortilla Flat, In Dubious Battle)* simply to rewrite the source, and the above plot outline does not do justice to the intricate elaboration of the Cain and Abel story, of which he wrote: "Without this story—or rather a sense of it—psychiatrists would have nothing to do. In other words this one story is the basis of all human neurosis—and if you take the fall along with it, you have the total of the psychic problems that can happen to a human." Although the key events of the story—the rejection and the murder (or near murder)—reoccur predictably, Steinbeck varies the personalities of his figures and their roles so as to amplify considerably the story's significance. Cyrus, the first Trask, appears alone and is by his initial description ("something of a devil") and actions a Cain figure. As father to Adam and Charles by two "Eves," the second called Alice, he represents the Adam of Genesis. As the rejecter of Charles's gift, he plays God. This identification of father and God (made explicit once by Adam) is repeated in the next generation; but then it is Adam Trask, the Abel figure of the previous enactment (who in the Bible has no issue), who is father of Caleb and Aron (one of whom, it is suggested, was begotten by Charles) and is thus also Adam of Genesis. This device of multiple roles is reinforced by confusing the associations expected of the names: Cyrus prefers Adam's qualities to those of Charles, whose mother's name was Alice; Adam is unreasonably infatuated with Cathy (pure evil), but Charles recognizes her Cain nature and hates her; both Cyrus and Adam prefer the "Abel" son; Caleb looks like Adam, and Aron not only looks like Cathy but, unlike his brother and despite his innocence, is capable of great violence; Abra, whose father, like Cyrus, is a thief, prefers Caleb to Aron. It is Adam and Aron who are exiles from their home, not Charles and Caleb. Furthermore, all three of the identical inheritances— one hundred thousand dollars—in the novel descend from Cain figures—Cyrus, Charles, Kate. These two devices—multiple roles and confusion of qualities—provide the foundation for the book's minor and major premises: that every man is capable of all roles, and that every man is responsible ("Thou mayest") for choosing which role he will play in life.

Thus the significance of Caleb, the only Trask survivor, whose mixture of good and evil is indicated by the letters of his name—a combination of Cain *and* Abel. As in the Bible, Aron does not enter the Promised Land; but it is promised to Caleb by the Lord, "him will I bring into the land where into he went [Canaan]; and his seed shall possess it" (Numbers, 14:24). The name of his future wife, Abra, is but a slight change from Arba, or Hebron, the city that is given to Caleb "according to the commandment of the Lord unto Joshua" (Joshua 15:13). *East of Eden* suggests that pure goodness—

Adam's passiveness, Aron's excessive "purity"—is self-destructive. Although the victims of parental rejection may exercise violence, paradoxically it is they, out of their suffering and guilt, who are frequently the accomplishers. Just a few days before actually beginning work on his first draft of the novel, Steinbeck noted in his journal that he hoped to write of good and evil, strength and weakness, love and hate, beauty and ugliness, and tell "how these doubles are inseparable—how neither can exist without the other and of how out of their groupings creativeness is born."

Actually, Steinbeck pushes even farther. The reading that gives "Thou mayest rule over him [sin]" as the moral of the Cain and Abel story is extended in Part Four, through the speculations of Caleb and Lee, the Chinese servant of the Trask family, to deny the doctrine of original sin and assert man's free will in general. As Steinbeck demonstrates in *In Dubious Battle*, his extensive knowledge of the Bible was equaled by but not confused with his knowledge of *Paradise Lost*, in which God says of Adam, "I made him just and right, Sufficient to have stood, though free to fall" (III, 97–98). And in Book IX, "Within himself/The danger lies, yet lies within his power;/Against his will he can receive no harm" (348–350). Milton's intention was to reconcile man's free will with the fact of God's foreknowledge; Steinbeck's intention was to assert man's ability to choose good in spite of man's contemporary view of himself as "weak and sick and ugly and quarrelsome," as he wrote to his editor. The last word spoken in *East of Eden* is "Timshol," which Steinbeck prefers to translate as "thou mayest."

Unfortunately, these subtleties and complications are more than equaled by an obviousness, failure of strategy, and contradiction of theme unknown in Steinbeck's work before *Burning Bright.* Certainly the use of identifying initial letters, along with the rejection of one brother's gift and his ensuing violence upon the preferred brother, would seem to provide more than ample signs to even the dozing reader. But although Samuel and Lee explicitly reject the names Cain and Abel for the boys, Caleb and Aron are chosen only after a reading and discussion of the fratricide story in Genesis. As the rejected gift of Cain was "of the fruit of the ground" and the accepted gift of Abel was "the firstlings of his flock," so the rejected gifts of Charles and Caleb are "agricultural" in source: a penknife bought with money from chopping wood, fifteen thousand dollars from the sale of beans. The gifts of Adam and Aron are "pastoral": a stray puppy, high examination scores through the help of (yes!) *Pastor* Rolfe of the Episcopal church. To his father's inquiry, after the "murder" of Aron, Caleb replies, "Am I supposed to look after him?" (In Genesis, Cain replies to God, "Am I my brother's keeper?") Steinbeck not only provides Charles with a scar that "looked like a long fingermark laid on his forehead," to remind us of the mark of Cain, but has him talk about it in terms echoing Genesis: "It just seems like I was marked." "I ought to be wandering around the world," he explains, "instead of sitting here on a good farm. . . ." Just before Adam

returns home and sees his brother's scar, he talks with a bar-
tender who is also marked and called Cat, which incident he
conveys to his brother. Cathy's mark, "like a huge thumb-
print," is even more obvious, and both she and Charles notice
each other's scar and identify each other as "devils." As devil
or Satan or Serpent (in addition to her Cain role) Cathy is
overburdened with signs: feet "almost like little hoofs," a face
"heart-shaped," small sharp teeth, flickering tongue, a preference for dark dens and the colors of a rattlesnake—"rust and
yellow." The scene in which she gives birth to the twins (as
easily as a snake lays eggs) is full of portents. A buried meteor
(fallen star, Lucifer) is discovered by Samuel just before the
birth, and is associated with a previous world destroyed. These
and many other such references evidence the author's belief,
expressed frequently in the *Journal*, that without glaring signs
critics as well as readers would miss "the great covered thing."
Ironically, and unfortunately, the state of Steinbeck criticism
at the time almost justified such a belief.

Despite the excessive and obvious parallels to Genesis, and
perhaps because of its discussion by all the major characters as
well as the author himself, the novel's theme is somewhat
blurred. Good is presented at various times as diametrically
opposed to evil, as a necessary complement, as merely a different aspect, and as the resultant product of evil. The terms are
even seen as relative, as when Lee says of Cathy that what she
is doing (operating the most perverted and depraved whorehouse in California) is "neither good nor bad." The author

himself says of the systematic decimation of the Indians in the nineteenth century, "It was not nice work but, given the pattern of the country's development, it had to be done." This kind of confusion is not abetted by the introduction of various speculations reminiscent of popular psychology handbooks: the dire effects of rejection and guilt, the sanity of love, etc. And when Steinbeck leaves the story to speculate at large ("this I believe") his ideas resolve into clichés, an essentially cracker-barrel philosophy. For Steinbeck has little of that talent for entertaining yet speculative thinking which was Aldous Huxley's genius as a novelist. Rather, he was a man of a few, sometimes profound, deeply *felt* ideas, and his talent never lay in talking about them (not even in *Sea of Cortez*, as we shall see), but in embodying them in passionate yet objective forms —even in the interchapters of *The Grapes of Wrath*.

Although the main drift in *East of Eden* is toward asserting belief in man's free will, both author and "spokesman" characters sometimes deny that belief at important points. Steinbeck's initial description of Cathy has her born a "monster," a "malformed soul," a statement he partially withdraws some hundred pages later; but the same quality is intuitively and immediately recognized by Charles, Lee, Samuel, and others. Although Cathy tries to hide her innate evil nature, it reveals itself at the slightest loss of control, such as results from a little alcohol. Lee, who speaks nothing but wisdom in the book, says near the end, "He [Adam] couldn't help it, Cal. That's his nature. It was the only way he knew. He didn't have any

choice. But you have. Don't you hear me? You have a choice."
Apparently, as in *Burning Bright*, some are less equal than
others. It is interesting to note here that not until he was more
than halfway through the first draft did Steinbeck come up
with the unusual translation of Genesis by a contemporary
Hebrew scholar which allowed him to make (with some grammatical violence) "Thou mayest rule over him [sin]" the novel's
moral fulcrum. Other translations render the passage "thou
shalt. . . ."

Finally, there is in *East of Eden* a failure in those professional skills without which any novelist is doomed: invention,
characterization, prose style, angle of vision, discipline. It is not
credible that Samuel should not see the Trasks for ten years,
that he should die on the Ides of March. It is not credible that
a group of elderly Chinese, the youngest over ninety-four,
should spend three years learning Hebrew in order to translate
one word (incorrectly) and then begin on Greek! The novel's
re-creations of the past are often set pieces of cultural nostalgia
suited to the pulp magazines—such as the bits about the
Model T Ford. We do not believe that a boy of Caleb's time
and age enters into partnership with five thousand dollars borrowed from a Chinese servant and turns it into a fifteen-
thousand-dollar profit, which he then methodically burns, a
thousand-dollar bill at a time, because his father would not
accept the money as a present. The account of Lee's birth, in
part similar to that in Bret Harte's "The Luck of Roaring
Camp," is not credible, nor his attending Berkeley for several

years, nor his smoking opium and drinking wormwood, nor his continuing servitude—at least not all of them together. In no other work of fiction did Steinbeck strive so hard to make his people vivid, unusual, arresting, endowing them with a life disproportionate to their function in the novel. Even the necessary nurse who is present for only two pages is grotesquely individualized.

Most indicative of Steinbeck's condition as a writer is not this failure at relatively new elements in his fiction but the failure of what had been one of his most consistent and remarkable talents: the felicity and variety of his prose. *East of Eden,* like *Burning Bright,* attempts a figurative language and a strange syntax sadly in contrast to the poetic realism or cold, hard spareness or burlesque archaism or impassioned rhetoric or plain style of his previous work. Instead, there are countless passages such as these: "Tom got into a book, crawled and groveled between the covers, tunneled like a mole among the thoughts, and came up with the book all over his face and hands"; "The coyotes nuzzled along the slopes and, torn with sorrow-joy, raised their heads and shouted their feelings, half-keen, half-laughter, at their goddess moon"; "a man's mind vagued up a little"; "all around the main subject the brothers beat."

Perhaps the most pernicious influence in *East of Eden* is the irresolute, arbitrarily changing function of the narrator and the nature of his voice. The narrator who begins the novel ("I remember . . .") becomes confused with the autobiographical

"I" and disappears for such long stretches of time that he becomes disassociated from the events of the novel. He does not seem to be necessary; nothing *results* because *he* is telling the story, and, as a very rare "me," and once "John," he is completely unimportant to that story, being, logically and historically, not even an observer of it. The novel soon escapes from the narrator's control, just as *Moby Dick* gets away from Ishmael. Furthermore, when the first-person narrator reappears, his "voice" is often so different from its last appearance as to destroy any sense of continuity.

In the mock discourse Steinbeck sent his editor (not used) to serve as "dedication, prologue, argument, apology, epilogue and perhaps epitaph all in one," "Editor" is presented as saying to "Writer," "The book is out of balance. The reader expects one thing and you give him something else. You have written two books and stuck them together." Other members of the publishing firm add further criticism, all of which is resisted by "Writer." Steinbeck's intention may have been facetious, but criticism of the novel while Steinbeck was working on it had been very real indeed, beginning with Pascal Covici's reaction to the very first chapters that Steinbeck completed and continuing intermittently to the end. One reader suggested Steinbeck "get on with the story and not stop for comment," and also "leave the Hamiltons out of the book." Harold Guinzburg, the president of the Viking Press, was reported "bewildered." These professional reactions to his novel annoyed and angered Steinbeck, so that he insisted repeatedly that he would hear no more of it as it was confusing him. He was not going to let criticism "change one single thing about the story or the method." The praise and approval he could not get from his publishers he received from his devoted wife, to whom he read aloud from the manuscript.

That Steinbeck did not listen to friendly and professionally competent criticism is not the issue here. As an artist, he was undoubtedly right to reject this "collaboration," as he once called it. But the epistolary journal that he kept while writing *East of Eden* provides an insight into the reasons why he persisted in justifying every aspect of the novel, why he did not trim the novel's sprawl but relished it, insisting that it contained all that he had been able to learn about his "art or craft or profession in all these years." After its publication, he wrote, "If *East of Eden* isn't any good then I've been wasting my time." Hemingway once said, quite in the midst of all those physical pleasures he so relished, that if he could not write, the rest would not be worthwhile. Steinbeck's *Journal of a Novel* is the painful record of a man seeing the sources of his artistic life drying up, hanging on in desperation to any straw that can provide the illusion of continued vitality, immersing himself in the very physical process of writing as if *that* might rekindle the vital flame, knowing that without that flame the rest was not worthwhile, thinking much of death—"It has been called the greatest gift."

In his *Journal*, Steinbeck compares the daily entries before writing on *East of Eden* to "a pitcher warming up to pitch—

getting my mental arm in shape." The analogy is a poor one, for the problems of a novel are different from those of a diary: pitching a baseball would be a bad warm-up for a soccer game. What happens eventually is that the journal and novel begin to fuse in subject matter and even prose style. Whole sentences from one find their way into the other. Necessary as Steinbeck found these warm-up letters, his dependence upon communication with Pascal Covici was not satisfied by them. Frequently he records being unable to begin or continue writing because Covici is out of the office or has not returned from a trip as promised. "You are not at your desk. I wonder where you are. . . . Well I finally got you and it's about time too. And now I will be ready to work." "You aren't in your office. I know you are out for coffee. But I will have trouble starting until I can talk to you."

As he begins his journal, Steinbeck reminds Covici that the book has been "blocked" for a long time, that there had been false starts, wrong directions. This is associated with his second divorce, which resulted in psychological traumas he had not expected to survive; "every life-force was shriveling." Fortunately, Elaine Scott, whom he had met two years before, changed all that, he writes. He begins with confidence in his plan for the book. As he records at a later date, however, the wounds were still "gangrenous," and could "break out destructively."

Steinbeck's intentions as he began work on *East of Eden* were to make the writing "spare and lean," void of every trick and simple enough in its difficulty to be understood by a child. He planned to comb through the first draft and remove even what few adjectives might have slipped in. Just ten days into the writing, he wants to use "every bit of technique I have learned consciously" and also "let it go unconsciously." The book is to be "not a novel but an history. And while its form is very tight, it is my intention to make it seem to have the formlessness of history." Three weeks later, "And in pace it is much more like Fielding than like Hemingway." From this point, all of his intentions are toward increased looseness, easier pace, greater comprehensiveness. He abandons all attempt at "restricting form in an iron cast." Two weeks after that, the book is to be about "everything"; he will "indulge every instinct," use "every method, every technique." Soon he is talking about his "great sprawling book" and its proliferation, how "everything has pups." Finally he justifies himself on the grounds that perhaps "a long book, even not so good, is more effective than an excellent short book"!

On April 24, Steinbeck writes, "Sometimes the old terror comes up in the night but thank goodness it is pretty much gone in the daytime, *except right at first and not every day then*" (italics added). With this everything falls into place. Not only the book's sprawling materials, the necessity to begin each workday with a stint at his journal, and the compulsive nature of his need to communicate with his editor, but his frequently stated disinclination to move his novel toward an ending: "But I'm very glad the book is not finished—I would hate to have it done. I don't like to think of the time when it is done. That will be a bad day for me. A real bad day." Two months later, "I do not know what I will do when it is finished. I will have some difficulty in living. I think there will be a bad time. . . ." He is "terrified to write finish on the book for fear I myself will be finished." In the last month of work, he hits upon a plan for a second volume and seems to take much courage from it. Yet suddenly, while on the very last chapter, he again balks completely and insists, "No time limit now. I may go on all year."

Of course *East of Eden* was completed, but from this point Steinbeck simply "went on" for most of the remaining seventeen years of his life.

THE WINTER OF OUR DISCONTENT

Steinbeck's recurrent statement while writing *East of Eden* that "there is nothing beyond this book—nothing follows it" seems fulfilled in the next two novels that he published: *Sweet Thursday* (1954) and *The Short Reign of Pippin IV* (1957), typed by reviewers as, respectively, "good fun" and "frothy extravaganza." It was not until nine years after *East of Eden* that he again attempted to write seriously about a serious theme, returning in *The Winter of Our Discontent* (1961) to the economic realities of modern society treated so variously in *Cannery Row, The Pearl,* and *The Wayward Bus,* but with a moral vision considerably more complicated and uncertain than his pronouncement, in *East of Eden,* about man's freedom to choose between good and evil.

The complications are foreshadowed by the novel's title, which applies the words of Shakespeare's villainous Richard III to a sequence of events which, although obviously parallel to Christ's Betrayal, Crucifixion, and Resurrection, constitute ironic inversions of them. The protagonist of the book is Ethan Allen Hawley, a "just under forty" Harvard graduate, a Mason, a descendant of two powerful, distinguished New England families, and presently a grocery clerk in the town of his ancestors, where he lives with his wife Mary and two children. The plot is essentially the story of his rise from penury and civic unimportance to wealth and political influence, a rise he accomplishes by abandoning his own principles of honesty and embracing the accepted ethics of the business world, epitomized by Mr. Baker, the banker. In the process, encouraged by Margie (a fortuneteller) and Morphy (a clerk at the bank), he causes the death of his friend Danny, gives and takes bribes, turns informer on his employer Marullo, and almost robs a bank. Meanwhile his son, Ethan Allen, Jr., also succeeds, temporarily, by plagiarizing his winning "I Love America" essay, but is exposed to the contest sponsors by his younger sister, Ellen. The novel ends with Ethan Hawley's abortive attempt at suicide.

In his concern over *East of Eden,* Steinbeck had theorized in his daily journal that the novel was falling in popularity before the onslaught of nonfiction because the form had not changed much since Sherwood Anderson. The new freedoms, looseness and relaxations in form and style in which he was then indulging, were rationalized on this basis as an alternative to the well-made novel, in the hope that his new kind of fiction "might find a public ready for the open and honest." That such a public indeed existed was proved by the popular reception of his long novel. Thus encouraged, Steinbeck continued to relax his style in *The Winter of Our Discontent.* The novel is told in a mixture of third- and first-person narration, the former neatly but for no apparent reason confined to the first two chapters of each of the novel's two parts. Furthermore, whereas the first two chapters are so dramatically presented that one is scarcely aware of the third-person narrator, the first two chapters of the second part present a narrator who is very much present and who is difficult to distinguish, after 150 pages of first-person narration, from Ethan Hawley himself. And Steinbeck does not use the first-person narrative form in order to employ its subtleties and complexities—its simultaneous relationships to author, narrator, reader, and material— nor to better reveal character. Rather, Steinbeck seems to use the first-person voice to indulge his own loquaciousness, to harangue the reader through various interior monologues and soliloquies delivered ostensibly by Ethan Hawley. The reader familiar with Steinbeck recognizes these "Hooptedoodles," as they are called in *Sweet Thursday,* to be characteristic of the author's recent thinking. They suggest that Steinbeck the novelist has given way to Steinbeck the Sage, the Guru. They are made even more obtrusive by their context, for in this novel perhaps more than in any other, he moves the action forward through dramatic, conversational scenes. This technique here results in the further disadvantage, especially in Part One, of requiring the characters to reveal in sometimes unrealistic conversations the necessary background which a more novelistic (narrative) technique could have easily provided.

In its prose style, also, *The Winter of Our Discontent* reflects the self-indulgence which Steinbeck had admitted as a new phase of his development in the *Journal*. He continues his attempt to write a figurative prose and "poetic" rhythm completely alien to his talents, a style he had wisely suppressed after his first novel, until its eruption in *Burning Bright*. A day changes in quality as it is "warped by a thousand factors of season, of heat or cold, of still or multi-winds, torqued by odors, tastes, and the fabrics of ice or grass, of bud or leaf or black-drawn naked limbs." That this prose style is a device for characterizing the first-person narrator, Ethan Hawley, would be possible were it not also the prose style of those sections narrated in the third person by the author himself. Steinbeck further confuses himself with his main character when in his third-person narratives he frequently breaks from his established past tense into the present tense of Ethan's monologues: "The old Phillips house in the second block *is* a boarding house now." Similarly, Ethan is confused with the author: "A single un-shaded light *hung* from a roof beam. The attic is floored with. . . ." This is even more explicit when Ethan lectures on the craft of fiction, every point a repetition of Steinbeck's published statements.

Another characteristic of Steinbeck's new style in *The Winter of Our Discontent*, a more successful one, is its plethora of quotations and allusions—nursery rhymes, folklore, fairy tales, popular songs, literature, the Bible, historical statements, and advertising slogans, all justified by Ethan's "useless" education in belles-lettres at Harvard. The novel even contains two quotations in Anglo-Saxon which give important clues to Ethan's plans, and several allusions to T. S. Eliot's *The Wasteland*—from a Tarot deck of cards to the lack of rain. Sometimes these allusions suggest a parallel to Hamlet in his predicament—the impulse to act stalemated by moral scruple. And Ethan, like the Dane, sometimes in a tone of suppressed hysteria, unburdens his heart through words, which also veil his thoughts and cover his plans.

Indeed, the novel contains many allusions to Shakespeare. The title, quoted twice in the novel, is from the first words of *Richard III*, spoken by Richard himself. Some similarities between the two works can be drawn. Both Richard and Ethan, spurred, respectively, by physical and social disorder, scheme to improve their positions. Richard causes Clarence's imprisonment as part of his plans; Ethan causes Marullo's deportation. Richard's murder of his brother Clarence is like Ethan's "murder" of his "brother" Danny; Clarence is literally drowned in wine and Danny figuratively in whiskey. There are also allusions to *Macbeth*. Ethan, too, is a good and loyal person at the

beginning, but lets the prophecies of witches (Margie, Morphy, Baker) and his wife's ambitions influence him to "murder" his leader—Marullo, and then Danny, who proceeds to
haunt Ethan's dreams and even a festival supper like Banquo's
ghost. Even more obvious are Ethan's four allusions to *Antony
and Cleopatra* when addressing his wife—as precise as, "You
must come to Rome! Egypt isn't big enough for you." Ethan,
too, sacrifices his honor and duty. Other easily recognized
allusions to or borrowings from Shakespeare include *Richard II*
and *Romeo and Juliet.*

Although altogether these allusions do not generate the
novel's theme (nor its structure), in their number and variety
they do serve effectively to amplify it, and, together with the
novel's pervasive presence of folklore and popular culture, to
place that theme in a richer context. The two most important
sources of allusion and borrowings, however, are the Fourth of
July and the New Testament, particularly the events of Passion
Week. The novel begins with Ethan's awakening on Good
Friday morning and is half over by Easter Monday. From this
point, time is telescoped to the Fourth of July weekend, which
takes up the last quarter of the book, again concluding on
Monday. These two holidays in their respective moral and
patriotic, individual and national substance, provide the structural poles of Steinbeck's novel.

This use of structuring sources in *The Winter of Our Discontent* is, as usual in Steinbeck's fiction, creative rather than
imitative. Ethan Allen Hawley embodies all three of the major

figures of the Passion. He is Christ in his initial morality and unworldliness; he plays Judas to this Christly aspect of himself for money; he is also Pontius Pilate in his judgment of this Christ self, complete to a modern version of "What is Truth?" when he says, "If the laws of thinking are the laws of things, then morals are relative too, and manner and sin—that's relative too in a relative universe."

The events of the Passion are similarly transformed. Good Friday becomes the day of Ethan's "temptation": Pride (Baker's appeals to his ancestral heritage), the Flesh (Margie's proposition) and the World (Bigger's bribe). The last of these is offered between noon and three o'clock in the afternoon (the sixth and ninth hours after sunrise) while Ethan is in his closed, darkened store commemorating Christ's three hours on the cross. His falling into temptation is ensured by a variety of forces. Margie predicts his future—"Everything you touch will turn to gold"—and urges him to live up to it. Marullo comes to instruct him in business ethics "so that for the first time Ethan understood it." Morphy, whose name and history suggest the infinite forms of the devil, not only lectures him upon the legality and normality of accepting Bigger's bribe, but teaches him the feasibility of both robbing the bank and getting Marullo deported. At home, Ethan's wife and children complain of their poverty and social position. He does not succumb to temptation until the small hours of the morning on Saturday, "the only day of the world's days when He is dead." In an interior monologue of sixteen pages, conducted mostly in a dark cave (sepulcher), Ethan reviews his own life, his ancestors and their wealth, the failure of his father and himself, and the business lessons of Good Friday. Although making no overt decisions at this time, he comes to accept the principles necessary for worldly success.

Thus, unlike that of Christ, Ethan's descent into Hell accomplishes his damnation in moral terms, but his salvation in terms of the world. At work a few hours later, he recapitulates his monologue and concludes that "where money is concerned the ordinary rules of conduct take a holiday." Throughout that day he is noted to be "different" and "not like the same man" by Margie, Marullo, and Mr. Bigger. His having succumbed to the devil's temptations is formalized that same evening by the "witch" Margie, who has a vision of Ethan as a rattlesnake changing its skin, and Ethan undergoes an inverse "conversion" experience described by himself as like a possession by the devil.

Easter Sunday morning begins with Ethan patting his wife's "silk-covered fanny" and saying, "Kyrie eleison!" They go to church and hear "the news announced that Christ was risen indeed." That day the ironically arisen Ethan confers shrewdly with Baker, high priest of business, about his financial future and decides definitely to rob the bank, get Marullo deported, and take possession of Danny's valuable property by providing him with the means of suicide—money for alcohol. Part One ends on the Monday after Easter with Ethan furthering all his plans for gaining the world he has bought with his soul.

These inversions of the Passion are supported by a casual but rich texture of details and references. Throughout Good Friday Ethan recites passages pertinent to the hour from the Passion according to St. Luke. The Judas theme in the novel is ubiquitous and appears not only in Ethan's betrayal of himself, but in his betrayal of Marullo, Baker, and Danny, whom in a dream he kisses on the mouth. It also appears in Ellen's betrayal of her brother; Margie's betrayal of Mary (when she attempts to seduce Mary's husband); Baker's betrayal of the town council; and the police chief's betrayal of both.

In *East of Eden*, Steinbeck had suggested that the story of Cain and Abel together with that of the Fall were, historically or symbolically, quite enough to account for the human condition. There are many little details which suggest Ethan's fall at the urging of his vapid, insipid, ironically named wife (Mary), whom, as Adam does Eve in *Paradise Lost*, he considers much too highly, even praying to her on one occasion. The Cain theme is obviously present in Ethan's "murder" of Danny: "I am my brother Danny's keeper and I have not saved him"; "I feel I should be my brother Danny's keeper." Like Caleb in *East of Eden*, Ethan has inherited both good and evil —pirates on one side of his family and pilgrims on the other.

As the Easter weekend provides the moral and individual pole of reference in *The Winter of Our Discontent*, so the Fourth of July weekend provides the novel's patriotic and national pole. Unlike the Passion, Independence Day is not exploited in detail, but rather used as a symbol of national ideals.

The Fourth of July weekend provides the chronology for only the last quarter of the book, but the ideals it represents are examined throughout. Ethan Allen Hawley's ancestors came over on the *Mayflower*, and their important role in shaping the nation's history is frequently recalled by him. He is named for one of them. His grandfather and great-aunt Deborah, embodying respectively Yankee shrewdness on the one hand and love of learning and Christian precepts on the other, also reflect the heritage of both Ethan and the nation. Even Marullo, although an illegal immigrant, came full of our national ideals, having memorized the words on the Statue of Liberty, of the Declaration of Independence, and of the Bill of Rights. Yet in his life as an American he epitomizes the decline from these ideals to more real and practical axioms: "A guy got to make a buck! Look out for number one!" "Everybody does it," "Money gets money." The decline is further illustrated by Ethan's son, Allen, who on Good Friday decides to enter the "I Love America essay" contest and who on the Fourth of July is announced as the winner of an Honorable Mention. But on the next day, the last of the novel, he is discovered to have no ideals of his own, having plagiarized his "patriotic jazz" from the founding fathers. His sister's act of betrayal is morally ambiguous at best, and the boy's self-defense to his father, which would have been merely impertinent on Good Friday, is tellingly effective after Ethan's own "resurrection" on Easter Sunday: "Everybody does it. . . . I bet you took some in your time. . . ." It is after this exchange that

Ethan equips himself with razor blades and leaves to commit suicide in his cave.

That at the last moment he avoids suicide, he explains—most unsatisfactorily for the theme of the novel—by the fact that he must return a talismanic stone to his daughter, "its new owner. Else another light might go out." That the talisman could not prevent his own light from going out, turning to what he calls "a black wick," a "dark derelict," does not enter into his decision. Nor is there any hint here as to whether he will continue in his new, practical ethics and morality or give up his material gains and return to virtuous poverty or, most probably, both keep his gains and return to virtue, as his ancestors had done. In this respect, the novel's ending is not a satisfactory conclusion to the questions that have been raised. At best, we are asked to believe that the stone has power to keep Ellen Hawley from contamination in the midst of corruption and dishonesty, ranging from her own family to the national scene, a power that the novel, despite its several discourses about and manifestations of "magic" (Margie's cards, the narwhal cane, etc.) does not adequately support.

That Steinbeck should have settled for this indeterminate and unsatisfactory ending is particularly puzzling as the novel itself clearly develops the ground for a more positive position which he avoids as a concluding statement. For in addition to the Christian allusions, and working parallel to them, *The Winter of Our Discontent* embodies also important elements of Jungian psychology: the conscious mind, or Ego; the personal unconscious; and especially the collective unconscious with its archetypes. Ethan's sustained "night thoughts," or reveries on his nights of insomnia, especially in "the Place," his watery cave, are clearly descents into the personal and collective unconscious, as described by Ethan himself in Jungian terms: "This secret and sleepless area in me I have always thought of as black, deep, waveless water, a spawning place from which only a few forms ever rise to the surface. Or maybe it is a great library where is recorded everything that has ever happened to living matter back to the first moment when it began to live." Ethan's cave (an earth-altar archetype) is a place where he can, by sacrificing the conscious mind—"it isn't thinking I do there"—gain access to his deeper springs of being and take strength from them. The three nights he recalls spending in the cave—before entering military service, before marriage, and before the birth of his son—are clearly rites of passage or initiation archetypes, and his descent into the cave during the Easter weekend is the same. As before, he must ritualistically in his mind reconstruct the old harbor and lose his present identity, before he can submit himself to what he calls "that Congress in the Dark" and "the dark jury of the deep."

The result of this submission is that he emerges with a truer knowledge of himself and a new direction which "must have worked itself out in the dark place below my thinking level," coming "not as a thought but as a conviction." That knowledge is a threshhold experience. It enables him to dismiss his father as a "fool"; accept his ancestors as "treacherous, quarrelsome, avaricious"; approve of Marullo's business lesson; and assert that the "eaters" are not "more immoral than the eaten" because "in the end all are eaten." Ethan Hawley's final knowledge is that "money is necessary to keep my place in a category I am used to and comfortable in," and that the getting of money is, as his revered grandfather tells him in a vision, "no different" than it ever was. In other words, Ethan finds in his unconscious the necessary survival drives, which had atrophied in his conscious, genteel mind, and he becomes a transformed or "cured" personality no longer at the mercy of contradictory impulses, but in possession of a strong ego capable of mediating effectively between his unconscious and the world in which he lives.

Clearly, the moral carried on this level of the narrative is counter to that carried by the allusions to Christ's Passion as discussed above. Yet it is based on the same events and structure. By his ambivalent, inconclusive ending, Steinbeck shows himself in his last novel as still balancing between the values derived from scientific, nonteleological "Is-thinking" ("What happens is right for me," says Ethan, "whether or not it is good.") and those derived from a mystic or religious view of human life. This balance has always been present to a lesser or greater degree in his writing. In his best work it is alive and creative. In *The Winter of Our Discontent*, however, despite the richness of texture, it is static. The dead nature of this balance and the declining command of language and invention result in one of his weaker serious novels.

8

❋❋❋❋❋❋❋

Other Short Fiction:
The Long Valley, The Moon Is Down,
Sweet Thursday, The Short Reign of Pippin IV

ALTHOUGH PUBLISHED thirty years before his death, *The Long Valley* (1938) contains almost all of Steinbeck's short stories. He was to publish only some half dozen more during his lifetime, none of which measures up to the level of those in this collection. In view of the episodic tendency of his early novels *(The Pastures of Heaven, Tortilla Flat)* Steinbeck's interest in the short story is not surprising, nor is their variety of form and subject matter. In fact, with very little change "The Murder," "The Harness," and "Johnny Bear" might become chapters in *The Pastures of Heaven.* Another story, "The Raid," clearly springs from the same source as *In Dubious Battle* and might have easily been included in that novel. The short sketch

"Breakfast" was actually incorporated into *The Grapes of Wrath* (chapter twenty-two). "The Snake," in its setting and in its major character, Dr. Phillips, looks forward to *Cannery Row* and could have served as one of that novel's interchapters. Three of the stories—"The Gift," "The Great Mountains," "The Promise"—share common thematic materials, setting, and characters; grouped under the title *The Red Pony*, they had been reprinted in 1937. "The Leader of the People," also found in *The Long Valley*, although sharing the same setting and characters, was not printed as part of *The Red Pony* until that book's republication in 1945. They are surely among the finest stories of boyhood in American literature.

There remain only five stories, then, that are not either closely related to the novels or do not form a body of work in their own right. The most unusual of the five, "St. Katy the Virgin," needs only some good belly laughs for commentary. It attests to Steinbeck's reading in early literature, particularly Malory's *Morte d'Arthur*, which remained a lifelong interest. "Vigilante" touches upon the group-man concepts of *In Dubious Battle*, but is entirely different from that novel in its technique and its Freudian slant. "Flight," although having a Mexican-American family as its characters, has nothing else in common with *Tortilla Flat*. Finally, "The Chrysanthemums" and "The White Quail" are psychological studies of married but childless and sexually flawed or deprived females of a sort that Steinbeck did not again return to in his novels.

It is in fact striking the extent to which there appear in these stories a variety of disagreeable women. Only in *The Red Pony* stories, the "Breakfast" fragment, and "Flight" are there competent, child-bearing, relatively normal women. The wife in "Vigilante" is shrewish and domineering. Emalin Hawkins in "Johnny Bear" is so cold that she helps her pregnant but unwed sister to hang herself. In "The Harness," Emma Randall is a frigid and prematurely aged wife who uses her husband's guilt feelings over his sexual infidelity (once a year) to dominate him and keep him in harness. Mary Teller in "The White Quail" has a separate bedroom from her husband and keeps the door locked; her narcissism is symbolized by her prim garden. In "The Snake," with obvious sexual connotations, a woman pays for the privilege of watching a rattlesnake kill and swallow a rat. In "The Murder," Jelka becomes a loving and faithful wife only after her husband follows his father-in-law's advice and beats her with a whip. St. Katy of "St. Katy the Virgin" undergoes a religious conversion, lives a pious life, does good deeds, and is eventually made a saint, but ironically the story is a burlesque of medieval saints' legends; and besides the female in question is a sow! Throughout his fiction, Steinbeck seems to judge women by male chauvinist standards and, except for good mothers or perfect prostitutes, tends to find them inadequate or seriously neurotic.

The most sympathetic woman in these short stories is Elisa Allen of "The Chrysanthemums," who is not quite sure of her feminity. Her house, too, like that of Emma Randall, Mary Teller, and Jelka, is "hard-swept" and "hard-polished." Her frustrated motherhood is expended in the loving care of her chrysanthemums. She is almost excessively competent; there is something masculine about her gardening clothes and the flowers seem "too small and easy for her energy." The word "strong" to describe her is used several times—by herself and her husband as well as by the author. Her husband complains that she is always changing—"You've changed again." This sexual ambiguity is dramatically resolved by the "very big," older, bearded and graying itinerant pot-mender for whose way of life she expresses some curiosity and desire. Upon this father figure, who praises and admires her chrysanthemums, she releases a slightly disguised and embarrassing flood of sexuality. When, later, on the road into town with her husband, she sees where the pot-mender has thrown away the chrysanthemums he pretended to want and she had given him with such immodest pleasure, her sexual ambiguity returns. Steinbeck's early interest in psychology and the nature of female sexuality, perhaps showing the influence of D. H. Lawrence, is an interesting, though brief, phase.

Considering Steinbeck's eventual reputation as a "proletarian" or "protest" writer, and considering that the stories in *The Long Valley* were all written during the Great Depression, years of widespread unemployment, revolutionary politics, and violent labor demonstrations (the "angry decade" as it has been called), it is curious that only "The Raid" deals with any of these matters. Even this one story is clearly a part of his early plans for *In Dubious Battle,* the only novel concerning contemporary issues that he had written up to that time. The similarities extend from setting and characters to prose style: an agricultural small town, vigilante action, a pair of Communist labor organizers (one of them more experienced) with similar recollections—broken arms, broken jaws that doctors refused to tend.

Of special significance here is the extent to which "The Raid," in its use of Christian allusions and symbols, looks forward to their more elaborate application to the proletarian materials of *In Dubious Battle* and *The Grapes of Wrath.* Ironically, in "The Raid" as in *In Dubious Battle,* the organizers vehemently deny any parallel between their actions and Christian values. "You lay off that religion stuff, kid," says Dick. " 'Religion is the opium of the people.' " Like Casy of *The Grapes of Wrath,* Root shouts to his attackers, "You don't know what you're doing." Dick sponsors his younger companion, catechizes him, tests him, and will "present" him, very much as a convert. Root is cautioned to hate the sin but not the sinner—"They don't know no better." Martyrdom for the cause is viewed as a consummate goal, for "We're all brothers"; and they are encouraged by remembering (in reference to an unidentified portrait poster), "He wasn't scared. Just remember about what he did." When addressing the workers, their ignorance and awkwardness fall from them, and they become "somebody else, and the words came out like water out of a hydrant." The two organizers, fearful of vigilante action, setting up the paraphernalia for their labor meeting, by the light of oil lamps in an abandoned store—three apple boxes, some posters, leaflets and pamphlets—obviously parallel the early Christians, fearful of persecution, setting up portable, make-shift altars in the catacombs and ruins. The use of these allusions in "The Raid" emphasizes the significance of their more extensive use in the two novels that followed. Also retained in the two novels is the theme of conversion. Mack and Casy, like Dick, are sponsors, of Jim and Tom respectively. And all three neophytes undergo an ordeal—some form of symbolic death and rebirth—Tom in the cave, Root in the hospital room, Jim upon joining the Communist party.

"Flight," among the best of the short stories in *The Long Valley*, is, on one level, a simple one. A boy unthinkingly kills a man, takes flight, is pursued, and is himself deliberately killed. The writing is Steinbeck at his best—poetic in its rhythm and images, yet terse and realistic. On another level, however, it is a story of initiation, or perhaps *lack* of it. Most of the story concerns details of the boy Pepe's flight into the desolate granite mountains, where he finds that there is no escaping the consequences of having asserted his manhood—by resenting an insult and throwing his knife into a stranger as unerringly as earlier that same day he had playfully thrown it into a post. In his flight, he gradually loses his horse, his hat, and his gun, which are the heritage from his father and the trappings of civilization. So that at the end, entirely alone, escape hopeless and his right arm swelling with infection, he stands up in full view to take his pursuer's death shot with a dignity and purposeful courage that demonstrate he has found the true test of his manhood in death. Possibly, Pepe's failure to survive the advent of his manhood is related to the fact that he had not known his father and grew up in isolation with his mother and her younger children. He does not undergo a ritual preparation under the careful tutelage of an adult male, a sponsor; rather, with no preparation he is thrown from boyhood directly into an adult situation. Thus, unlike Root, Jim, and Tom, he does not undergo a rebirth, but rather returns entirely to the earth, which in the story's last sentence buries him in a little avalanche of broken rocks.

The theme of initiation present in "The Raid" and "Flight" finds its fullest expression in the short stories published under the title *The Red Pony*. Their setting is the Tiflin ranch in California, where the boy Jody lives with his father, mother, and Billy Buck, a hired hand. In the first story, "The Gift," Jody is given a red pony by his father; but, after the pony has become sick, he allows it to get out of the barn into a cold rain, where it dies with a circle of buzzards waiting. In the second story, "The Great Mountains," there arrives at the ranch an old Mexican named Gitano, who has returned to the environs of his birth, and that of his father, to die; but Carl Tiflin does not want the old man around, so Gitano steals an old worthless horse which Carl had considered shooting, and the two of them go off into the mountains to die together. Before going, however, the old man talks with Jody and shows him a beautiful Spanish rapier which had been handed down by his father.

In "The Promise," the third story, Jody is promised a foal by the mare Nellie if he will work for it and take care of everything connected with its birth—beginning with the breeding. The story ends with a difficult foaling in which Nellie must be killed in order to save her colt.

The initiation theme of these stories is clearly prepared for by Steinbeck's early stressing of Jody's childhood by various actions on his part that denote a lack of adult status: his not being allowed to shoot his rifle, the way he does his chores, etc. Yet, at the same time Jody feels "an uncertainty in the air, a feeling of change and of loss and of the gain of new and unfamiliar things." Steinbeck was well versed in Frazer's *The Golden Bough,* which contains a chapter on puberty rites, the ceremonies used by various cultures to mark the transition from childhood to adulthood. These ceremonies generally have certain elements in common. They begin with a separation of the boy from the mother and the world of childhood; this is often symbolized by a ritual death. There follows some ordeal to test the candidate's courage, after which he is for a period instructed in the sacred lore of his tribe. He then experiences a symbolic rebirth into the adult world. Although Steinbeck incorporated some version of all these elements, naturally they are not all part of one experience as they would be in a primitive culture. Rather, these elements are scattered over a period of time, as they are in other stories of initiation—Faulkner's "The Bear," Crane's *The Red Badge of Courage,* Hemingway's Nick Adams stories, etc.

Frequently, tribal initiations begin unexpectedly and with no indication of their purpose. Thus Jody is sent to bed one evening under circumstances which arouse his curiosity, for he feels his father has important news of some kind. But he is told, "Never you mind. You better get to bed." The following morning his father "crossly" commands him to accompany himself and Billy Buck to an unstated place for an unstated purpose. Jody "had trouble with his food then, for he felt a kind of doom in the air." His mother expresses concern that the men may keep him from school (childhood). That the men had just returned from taking cattle to be slaughtered perhaps adds to Jody's apprehension, for he is very sensitive to life and death symbols—the mossy spring and the cypress tree where hogs are butchered, which they pass on this significant morning. As an American Indian's ordeal might be to survive a period alone in the wilderness and bring back an eagle feather, Jody's task turns out to be that he must care for the red pony, which his father threatens to sell if Jody fails in any way, and during this period Jody "tortures himself" with fears of failing. The climax of this ordeal is to be the breaking of the pony "around Thanksgiving." Jody is very concerned that he not fail this test, and thinks of all the wrong things he could do, such as using his hands to stay on the bucking pony by grabbing the saddle horn. "Perhaps his father and Billy Buck would never speak to him again, they would be so ashamed." He also fears what the other boys will think if he does poorly—"it was too awful to think about." In a tribal community, failing the test could have such serious consequences as complete social ostracism. That this test never materializes and Jody is presented instead with a new and unexpected ordeal, the pony's sickness and death, is also a parallel to the pattern of initiation rites, in which boys are often deliberately misled as to the real nature of their ordeal.

In many cultures, the ordeal consists in part of some significant wound, usually circumcision. This Steinbeck accomplishes symbolically through the red pony with which Jody has become identified. (Frazer cites examples of such totem animals.) The description of the tracheotomy that Billy Buck performs on the pony is strikingly similar to that of a circumcision, and Jody feels all the terror and anxiety he would feel for himself. The death of the red pony, the totem animal, signifies the death of Jody as a boy. His courageous but "ignorant" fight with the buzzard which has started to eat his pony is the story's final learning experience, in which he becomes aware of the existence of death and evil in the world view which is his inheritance as an adult. As in many initiation rites, his face is daubed with blood.

It would probably be a mistake to see the whole of *The Red Pony* as illustrating the rites of initiation step by step and in sequence. But the general pattern is carried out in the remaining stories. "The Great Mountains" corresponds to that period in the boy's preparation, after his symbolic wound and during convalescence, in which he is taken into the custody of one or more elders or holy men and instructed in the adult mysteries. From Billy Buck, he has started to learn about horses; just what

Jody learns from Gitano is not so definite. But he asks many questions about "the great mountains," which symbolize the home of the dead. Most probably, from the story's ending, he not so much learns about what lies beyond death as develops the proper attitude of awe and wonder toward it. Before Gitano rides off on the old horse Easter, he allows Jody a brief glimpse of the ancient Spanish rapier, which corresponds to the tribe's secret and sacred object, about which the initiate must stay silent—"It would be a dreadful thing to tell anyone."

"The Promise" continues Jody's initiation rites, again through the tutelage of Billy Buck. His childhood has symbolically died with the red pony in the first story, "The Gift." "The Promise" provides a second stage in the instruction started in "The Great Mountains," and at the end of the story, as in most initiation rites, Jody is symbolically reborn—with a new foal. The continuity of this horse symbol in all three stories is important. In "The Promise" he is again confronted with death, that of the mare Nellie; but also with the mysteries of life—copulation, gestation, birth; and furthermore, with the relationship between the two—death as the price of life.

Originally, Steinbeck ended *The Red Pony* with this story, which, significantly, ends the horse symbolism also. In *The Long Valley*, "The Leader of the People" appears as a separate story. But because it has the same characters and locale as the other Jody stories and because there is a sense in which it continues Jody's "education," the story was in 1945 added as the fourth episode in *The Red Pony*. But it is not essentially about Jody as the other stories are. Rather, through a new character, the grandfather, Steinbeck poses the question of the meaning and place which the pioneer heritage should have in our time. Through the attitudes of the father, the mother, and Billy Buck toward the grandfather, who embodies that tradition, are revealed a variety of responses, none adequate: rejection, veneration, respect. It is only to Jody that the grandfather finally communicates the essence of the tradition: that it was not being "the leader of the people" or fighting Indians that mattered, but the spirit of "westering," the intense participation in a mass movement of humanity which hungered for new experience and discovery; that the frontier was not a geographic line but a mental outlook. Perhaps in Jody's generation the urges rejected by his parents might become again a moving force. Steinbeck was to write of it in *The Grapes of Wrath*.

THE MOON IS DOWN

Steinbeck's only piece of fiction about World War II was written before he himself had seen anything of that war, in fact even before the United States was precipitated into the conflict by the attack on Pearl Harbor, December 7, 1941. Of even greater consequence for *The Moon Is Down* (1942) is the fact that it followed immediately after he completed *Sea of Cortez*. Steinbeck's expedition with Ed Ricketts into the Gulf of California had been in part an escape not only from the public harassments attendant upon *The Grapes of Wrath*, but psychologically from his increasing preoccupation with imminent world catastrophe: "—a zombie war of sleep-walkers which nevertheless goes on out of all control of intelligence." From the Gulf of California, he can observe that "thousands of miles away the great bombs are falling and the stars are not moved thereby," no more than the world is affected by the decimation of the shrimp population off the Mexican coast. It is perhaps this mood of detachment combined with his lack of personal experience with the war in Europe that accounts for the curious failure of this second of his works in the play-novelette form, which came at the peak of his powers, his first piece of fiction to be published since *The Grapes of Wrath* three years before.

Although never explicitly stated, the setting of *The Moon Is Down* seems to be a small town in Norway during the Nazi occupation. Its characters are intended as representative of the democratic and totalitarian forces there engaged. The action reveals the scope and true meaning of that engagement. Steinbeck took the title for the book from *Macbeth* (Act II, scene i), but there seems to be no significant correspondence between the two works. "The moon is down," meaning in the play that it is the darkest time of night, is used by Steinbeck to suggest the moral and sociological darkness of Nazi-occupied Europe. That darkness, however, is seen as a temporary condition, for the book presents man's spirit as free by nature and insists that it is impossible "to break man's spirit permanently," even though that freedom results in laxness and disorder which make it easy prey for those who have exchanged freedom for efficiency: "By ten forty-five it was all over. The town was occupied, the defenders defeated, and the war finished." But these are the first words, not the last. That man's free spirit will prevail is not an article of faith but of logic. The book's central, but unstated metaphor is a biological one contrasting the survival value of a relatively unorganized, unspecialized organism with one highly specialized and rigidly organized. In the essay "About Ed Ricketts," which is part of *The Log from the Sea of Cortez,* written after *The Moon Is Down,* Steinbeck comments that "a too greatly integrated system or society is in danger of destruction since the removal of one unit may cripple the whole." In *The Moon Is Down,* Doctor Winter notes of the "efficient" invading people that "ten heads lopped off will destroy them, but we are a free people; we have as many heads as we have people . . . leaders pop up among us like mushrooms."

The most serious weakness of this play-novelette in praise of the free spirit of man is its abstract parable form. Although everyone reading the book or seeing the play or motion picture at that time found evidence to assume the situation to be that of Nazi-occupied Norway, the invaders and the invaded are as unspecified as possible so as not to detract from the play of *forces,* of ideologies, which is the book's true subject, the true protagonists of its parable structure. But *The Moon Is Down,* unlike *Of Mice and Men, In Dubious Battle,* and *The Pearl,* does not embody its forces in credible, sympathetic characters and is thus abstracted beyond our ability to concern ourselves emotionally. At the time of its publication, just three months after Pearl Harbor, with most of Europe under the Nazi heel, the book's reduction of human oppression and suffering to abstract forces was deeply resented by many, particularly since Steinbeck insisted, as he had in *In Dubious Battle*, on balancing the conflict as much as possible. In their lack of efficiency and order, the invaded are reduced to silliness by such details as the mayor's wife badgering her husband about the hair in his ears; the traitors among them, exemplified by Mr. Corell, believe the conquest is for "a better state and an ideal way of life"; and the conquerors are given dignity by being depicted as fallible human beings, victims of circumstance and history. The realities of the newsreel as well as the efforts of propaganda had led the public to expect more obvious heroics on the one hand and degenerate bestiality on the other.

Furthermore, whereas his earlier attempt in the play-novelette form *(Of Mice and Men)* had succeeded in fusing the requirements of both forms, play and novel, in *The Moon Is Down*, these lie side by side. The stage description and cast of characters are presented with the brief, spare directness of the script for a play, and the omniscient author narrates unplayable scenes, such as the description of the children finding the parachutes. Only in one or two places does Steinbeck succeed in moving the reader—the murder of the homesick Lieutenant Tonder, and the death of Mayor Orden, which is compared to that of Socrates.

SWEET THURSDAY

With four months of writing still to do on *East of Eden*, Steinbeck had already decided he would next write a comedy, possibly in play form. Yet frequently during this same period, as we have already seen, he also expressed the fear and conviction that *East of Eden* "might be my last book," that "there is nothing beyond this book—nothing follows it." In a sense there is no contradiction here, for *Sweet Thursday* (1954) was written expressly as the source for a musical comedy by Rodgers and Hammerstein, who began work on the libretto while the novelette was still in progress. Their adaptation, *Pipe Dream*, opened in New York in December 1955 and, although called a "flop" by *Variety*, ran for 246 performances. It might be possible to pass very lightly over the book were it not for its length—270 pages—containing much material not required for a libretto, and its explicit relationship to *Cannery Row*, beginning with the first sentence of its prologue: "One night Mack lay back on his bed in the Palace Flophouse and he said, 'I ain't never been satisfied with that book *Cannery Row*. I would of went about it different.' "

Mack's dissatisfactions are limited to the lack of chapter titles, too much narration and description as opposed to conversation and dramatic action, and the lack of clearly marked, set-aside "hooptedoodle" passages or chapters in which the author can "spin up some pretty words maybe, or sing a little song with language." In *Sweet Thursday* Mack's first two objections are corrected, but the "hooptedoodle," despite two chapters so marked, is as ubiquitous and difficult to distinguish as it is in its predecessor. The changes which really matter, both as a new quality in the work itself and as a signpost in Steinbeck's career, lie in the characters and situations.

That Steinbeck could have found it possible to reduce "the Virtues, the Graces, the Beauties" of *Cannery Row*, not to mention Doc himself (and thus Ed Ricketts), to the level of a musical comedy is in itself a significant indication of his changing values. But furthermore, many of the changes and much of the new material go far beyond the requirements of a musical comedy, resulting in something closer to Walt Disney cartoons than to *My Fair Lady*. Beginning with the first chapter, "What Happened in Between," we learn that Fauna came to Cannery Row to run the whorehouse fresh from successfully managing a midnight mission in San Francisco; that Mack traveled all over the western United States in his search for uranium, following a Geiger counter which was recording the radium dial on a girl's wristwatch; that Lee Chong fulfilled a lifelong ambition by buying a schooner, loading it with all the goods from his grocery store, and sailing off to trade in the South Seas; that his replacement, Joseph and Mary, made a successful career of growing quantities of marijuana in the public plaza of Los Angeles, despite efforts of the police to locate the source; that Whitey No. 2 tried to bring back from the war a quart jar of human ears—pickled in brandy. These sophomoric efforts to entertain the reader fall considerably below the level of humor in *Cannery Row*. The allusive chapter titles are no better: "Where Alfred the Sacred River Ran," "The Playing Fields of Harrow," "O Frabjous Day!"

But more significant are Steinbeck's authorial statements about Doc, who, like the other characters, has undergone a strange change—"in spite of himself, in spite of the prayers of his friends, in spite of his own knowledge." The "in spite" here is very significant. One aspect of these changes is Doc's feeling of dissatisfaction with his former carefree life, his now wanting to make some contribution to the "Great Ledger" of man's accomplishments. That Steinbeck appreciates this impulse as genuine and worthwhile is clear: "Man owes something to man." In his previous work, striving to repay that debt is an ennobling action, as for example, in Chapter Fourteen of *The Grapes of Wrath:* "The last clear definite function of man— muscles aching to work, minds aching to create beyond the single need—this is man.... For man ... grows beyond his work, walks up the stairs of his concepts, emerges ahead of his accomplishments." But in *Sweet Thursday*, Steinbeck asks, "What can a man accomplish that has not been done a million times before?" Serious work interferes with Doc's enjoyment of life, and the author agrees with Mack, Fauna, and Joe Elegant that Doc's projected scientific research is but a subli- mation of the more basic drive of romantic love, that voice from his "marrow," his "guts." At one point his "low mind" threatens him with "red burning," "rage," and of festering inside until it will make him "sick and crazy" if it is not indulged. He realizes that "thought is the evasion of feeling." Doc's research project is accordingly made fun of in every detail, from its title—"Symptoms in Some Cephalopods Approximating Apoplexy"—to its techniques, to its significance. Doc himself comes to see that he has nothing, that he has built up his work's importance like a "little man pretending to be a big man, a fool trying to be wise." And clearly the author agrees with Mack that "we got to help him not to write that goddam paper." Consequently, Doc realizes that Suzy, the reluctant but able prostitute, is somehow greater even than J. S. Bach, his most revered composer; that he himself can never be a "whole man" without her, but only live "a gray half-life" and mourn for her "every hour" of the rest of his life!

True to the spirit of musical comedy, Doc not only gets Suzy, but, via a research grant, a chance to complete his paper and read it before a learned society. It is instructive of the book's theme that the scientific instrument which Cannery Row buys for Doc turns out to be not a microscope—indispensable in his work—but a telescope with which to enjoy the stars.

The anti-intellectualism of *Sweet Thursday* goes beyond the needs of musical comedy, and is symptomatic of Steinbeck's own predicament. "Parallels Are Related," one of the chapter headings of the novel states, and indeed it is impossible to doubt that in Doc's disaffection with his work Steinbeck is portraying his own artistic crisis, his "Creative Cross" as another chapter is titled. His choice of *Cannery Row*, and especially of Doc, who had been modeled on the essential companion of his more creative years, as the source of materials for this purpose is fascinating. It can be nothing less than a purposeful act of destruction, a severing of the cord, an attempt at a redefinition of himself along less demanding lines. The book that followed is a commentary upon the success of that attempt.

THE SHORT REIGN OF PIPPIN IV

Steinbeck's return to the scenes if not the themes of *Cannery Row* was followed three years later by his second book with a European setting. But whereas in *The Moon Is Down* he had attempted to write about a real situation of which he had no first-hand knowledge, *Pippin*, although a pure "Fabrication"—as it is subtitled—in its characters and action, is set in Paris, where Steinbeck lived for a period of time during the mid nineteen fifties. Unfortunately, Steinbeck chose to limit his depiction of French customs to a rather low level of comedy, such as Mme. Heristal's scolding of the maid for adjusting the ventilation to avoid a cold rather than to benefit the cheese. Other observations, such as the (to Americans) unexpected rigid morality of Frenchwomen, the domestic frugality, and the national intolerance of other languages or badly spoken French, are simply trite.

Steinbeck's observations of the political realities of a coalition government, however, sometimes have an edge. Briefly, the story concerns a Chaplinesque Frenchman (Pippin) who, through an impasse among the numerous and ridiculous political parties ("Conservative Radicals," "Christian Atheists," etc.) finds himself crowned king of France as the sole descendant of a royal line obscure enough to be unobjectionable to anyone. Through the exercise of intelligence, honesty, and altruism he merely succeeds in making enemies of everyone and thus unites all the squabbling, selfish parties in bringing about the end of his reign. No one really wants the monarchy. The Communists support the restoration because it would be "a position to kick off from and, indeed, would speed up the revolution"; the Socialists support it because "a king would keep the Communists in check"; the Centrists (of both right and left!) vote for it because it would "curb both Socialists and Communists"; etc.

The incidents themselves, however, smack not so much of satire or comedy or even farce as of slapstick: M. Rumorgue, leader of the "Proto-Communists," leaves the meeting which is determining the next form of government and goes back to Juan-les-Pins on receipt of a telegram announcing that his "Poland China sow, named Anxious, had farrowed"; after Pippin IV makes his first and only speech, he turns to walk off the platform but "an open-mouthed page was standing on the edge of his purple and ermine-collared cape," which "ripped from his shoulders and fell to the floor, exposing the row of safety pins up the back of his tunic and the baggy crotch of the trousers flopping between his knees." All this is far from the bits of mordant humor in Steinbeck's earlier serious novels, the sustained burlesque of *Tortilla Flat*, the tender humor of *Cannery Row*, the Swiftian humor of *The Wayward Bus*. It is a return to the level of stuff he had published as an undergraduate in the *Stanford Lit* under the pseudonym of Amnesia Glasscock.

The Short Reign of Pippin IV has its serious moments—for example, Pippin's reflections on the virtues of a quiet solitary life—but too often these lapses from slapstick are long disquisitions by Tod Johnson, son of "the egg king of Petaluma" (California), who teaches Pippin IV practical politics by lecturing him on the American social and political scene. He is an obvious mouthpiece and out of key with the other characters —Uncle Charles, Sister Hyacinthe, Pippin's wife Marie, and their daughter Clotilde—who seem created for a Walt Disney family comedy. Finally, Pippin's obviously serious seven-point speech which is found to be so shockingly innovative that he is forced to flee for his life during the revolution that follows it—well, that speech, dealing with wage-and-price control, housing, taxes, and "the break-up of large land-holdings to restore the wasted earth to productivity," contains nothing the French had not already had for a long time.

Like *Sweet Thursday*, which it resembles in the inaneness of its comedy, *The Short Reign of Pippin IV* contains certain resemblances to Steinbeck's earlier fiction. But again like the previous novel, these resemblances have an air of self-parody. As Fauna comes from a street mission to manage a whorehouse, Sister Hyacinthe comes to her convent after a career as nude entertainer at the Folies-Bergère—because her arches have fallen; like Joseph and Mary and Lee Chong, Uncle Charlie is a marginal but philosophical storekeeper; the various wise hermits from Merlin to the Seer of *Sweet Thursday* are recalled in the old man who pulls statuary out of the moat. Certain Steinbeck motifs are similarly recalled, to the same effect of parody—race memory, group man, the essentially uninteresting nature of marital relationships, biological determinism, unexplained periods of general good or evil, and so on.

The stagnation evidenced by the humor, characters, and situations is rivaled by the stagnation of ideas. As in *Sweet Thursday*, the movement of Steinbeck's protagonist is toward relapse. Doc, after some struggle with himself, settles back into a more comfortable conventionality; Pippin returns cheerfully to his quiet life of amateur astronomer. The telescope is significant in both novels, and both novels satirize a scientific essay. M. Rumorgue works not with cephalopods but with red clover. The title of his essay, however, is parallel to Doc's: "Tendencies and Symptoms of Hysteria in Red Clover." Perhaps (along with the telescope) apoplexy and hysteria are also significant clues. Eighteen years earlier, Casy discovered that "There ain't no sin and there ain't no virtue. There's just stuff people do. It's all part of the same thing. And some of the things folks do is nice, and some ain't nice, but that's as far as any man got a right to say." And it was a dynamic idea that led him to a vision of the brotherhood of man, the oversoul, and to a martyr's death. Now, the same words, spoken by the Seer who pulls statues out of the moat—a nice symbol—serve to announce a philosophy of simply drifting, for there is nothing to be done. Pippin sees "no reason for either hemlock or cross." Men are seen as "children or old," nothing in between. One can, like the old man, today pull out statues that will be thrown back in tomorrow, or one can get a telescope and look at the stars.

9

✦·✦·✦·✦·✦·✦·✦

Sea of Cortez,
Travels with Charley,
and Other Nonfiction

THE NONFICTION which Steinbeck has written varies widely in quality and subject matter. Furthermore, these variations correspond generally to the fluctuations of his fiction. His articles on migrant labor ("Dubious Battle in California," "The Harvest Gypsies" series, and two other pieces) have in common with *In Dubious Battle* and *The Grapes of Wrath* a high level of accomplishment as well as their materials. They remain the best of his short nonfiction.

Of the longer works, *Sea of Cortez* (1941) is in itself the most interesting, and the most valuable for its discussion of some important ideas embodied in Steinbeck's fiction. It was written in collaboration with Edward F. Ricketts, with whom he had undertaken a research trip into the Gulf of California. The trip had been conceived late in 1939 when Steinbeck, who had recently become a partner in Ricketts' Pacific Biological Laboratories, accompanied Ricketts on a specimen collecting expedition to the coast north of San Francisco. It was also in that year that Ricketts, who had left the University of Chicago without a degree after three years, published, in collaboration with Jack Calvin, *Between Pacific Tides*, a handbook of marine life along the Pacific shores of the United States. This book, innovative and advanced in its methods, has remained a standard in its field, continuously in print through several editions. It's somewhat technical and very functional Introduction was written by Steinbeck.

Had Steinbeck been merely a writer and Ricketts merely a scientist, it is doubtful that such a strong relationship would have developed between them. The figure of Doc in *Cannery Row*, although lacking certain important characteristics (curiously not supplied in Steinbeck's "About Ed Ricketts" written six years later) is an acceptable beginning for an understanding of Ricketts' character. To appreciate the extent of Ricketts' collaborative role in *Sea of Cortez*, however, it is necessary to know not only of his scientific work, such as *Between Pacific Tides* and numerous unpublished studies, but also that his literary, musical, and philosophical sophistication went far beyond the simplicities of his fictional portrait. He was a friend and correspondent of some impressive figures such as Joseph

Campbell and Henry Miller, as well as familiar with the colony
of bohemian intellectuals with whom Steinbeck consorted.
Philosophically, he can be described, in part, as a "naturalistic
mystic"—one whose feeling of kinship with the cosmic whole,
whose sense of awe, is achieved through the facts of science
and the truths of nature, rather than through the inward contemplation typical of traditional mysticism. To a large extent
this is also true of Steinbeck. Both men, however, reinforced
the naturalistic sources of their mysticism with selective reading in philosophy, religion, and psychology.

Ostensibly, *Sea of Cortez* is a day-by-day account of a six-
week specimen-collecting trip to the Gulf of California in
March and April of 1940, preceded by an account of the
motivations and preparations for such an undertaking. What
makes this book of fascinating interest, however, are the numerous passages of informal speculation, some quite extended,
to which the events of the journey give rise. It is divided into
two major parts, the "Narrative" and the "Phyletic Cata-
logue," but it must not be assumed that Steinbeck, the writer,
did the former and Ricketts, the scientist, did the latter. Both
men repeatedly resisted such identification. "It is a true compi-
lation [sic] in every sense of the word," wrote Ricketts; and
Steinbeck replied to his editor's plan to credit the authors
separately, that he found the suggestion "outrageous" and that
he "forbid" it because the book was "the product of the work
and thinking of both of us." Later, in his sketch "About Ed
Ricketts," Steinbeck described the continuous game of "specu-

lative metaphysics" in which he and his friend engaged, saying that they worked so closely together that he did not know in some cases who had started a particular line of speculation; "the end thought was the product of both minds." Yet, although one can accept this statement for the purpose of comparing the ideas in *Sea of Cortez* to Steinbeck's fiction in a general way, an examination of the book's history of composition suggests certain refinements.

From further statements by both men and from an examination of the manuscripts, it is clear that Steinbeck did the actual writing of the narrative portion, but that most of the text derives closely from a forty-six page, single-spaced, typed transcription of a journal of the expedition kept by Ricketts. Steinbeck had this in hand while writing; he himself had not kept a journal. As Ricketts put it, with admiration, "He takes my words and gives them a little twist, and puts in some of his own beauty of concept and expression and the whole thing is so lovely you can't stand it." Sometimes, however, Steinbeck follows Ricketts almost verbatim for extended passages. This is not to say that Steinbeck merely revised the journal; but the bulk of raw material derives directly from it. Furthermore, the book's most significant chapter, the Easter Sunday "sermon" (March 24), incorporates, with a few merely grammatical and syntactical changes, a twenty-page unpublished essay by Ricketts called "Non-teleological Thinking." In addition, the Ricketts journal itself contains numerous passages paraphrased from other of his unpublished essays.

Steinbeck's hand is much more importantly evident in the larger shaping of the book. Essentially, Steinbeck took a collection of field notes and random thoughts and gave them an aesthetic form which expressively embodies their import. "The design of a book," wrote Steinbeck on the first page, "is the pattern of a reality controlled and shaped by the mind of the writer." This simple statement gives a clue to the book's place alongside Thoreau's *Walden* and Hemingway's *Green Hills of Africa* as imaginative reconstructions of experience rather than mere journalistic recordings. Not least important in this shaping is what of Ricketts' material and personal recollections Steinbeck *left out*. For example, although his wife, Carol, was on the trip and appears in Ricketts' journal, she is not mentioned in the narrative; and omitted completely is any account of the return trip from the Gulf to Monterey. These and other details had no part in Steinbeck's careful design. Conversely, where Ricketts begins his journal as they pass Point Sur, leaving Monterey, Steinbeck precedes this with four chapters concerning the genesis of the trip and its preparations. These four chapters not only create the proper expectations but, with the material omitted at the end and some internal telescoping, serve to stretch out the actual chronology so that the important "sermon" on nonteleological thinking which is the book's philosophical center comes on Easter Sunday, exactly in the book's center although only one fourth of the collecting stations have been covered by that time.

Steinbeck emphasizes the circularity of his departure-arrival-departure pattern by certain accents. The voyage begins as the *Western Flyer* leaves the sheltered waters of Monterey Bay and enters the open sea. The boat is greeted by a flock of pelicans and a sea lion who looks like the old man of the sea himself; aboard ship, "the forward guy-wire of our mast began to sing under the wind, a deep and yet penetrating tone." The voyage ends as they leave the Gulf of California, at which time "a crazy literary thing happened. As we came opposite the Point there was one great clap of thunder, and immediately we hit the great swells of the Pacific and the wind freshened against us. The water took on a gray tone." And the last words in the book: "The big guy-wire, from bow to mast took up its vibration like the low pipe on a tremendous organ. It sang its deep note into the wind." These accents mark the limits of a mythic voyage, in quest of new knowledge, to an unknown sea.

Within this frame the book is shaped by the free flow of varied observations, incidents and speculations, and the inflexibilities of time and tide. Steinbeck's discourse on steering in chapter five, at the beginning of the voyage, becomes an image of their quest—"the working out of the ideal [a compass point] into the real [a destination]" and of "the relationship between inward and outward, microcosm to macrocosm." As they move along the shores of the Gulf between high and low tides, picking up specimens, comparing, examining, so the book's thought moves along the shores of human society, picking up specimens of thought and deed, comparing, examining. The little intertidal societies and the human society become manifestations of common principles, so that finally "all things are one thing and that one thing is all things—plankton, a shimmering phosphorescence on the sea and the spinning planets and an expanding universe, all bound together by the elastic string of time."

To give all the philosophical sources of this and other speculations, where possible to detail further the distinct contributions to the book of each collaborator, and to draw the correspondences between certain passages of *Sea of Cortez* and Steinbeck's other works is a task far beyond the limits of this book. Only some suggestions can be made. The clearest philosophical influences on *Sea of Cortez* are, appropriately, those of naturalist and evolutionary philosophers: W. C. Allee, with whom Ricketts had studied at Chicago and whose book, *Animal Aggregations,* contains parallels to Steinbeck's "group-man" concept; William Emerson Ritter *(The Natural History of Our Conduct),* zoologist at Berkeley, whose organismal conception of the universe is extensively paraphrased in *Sea of Cortez,* as in the passage quoted above; Jan Smuts *(Holism and Evolution);* Robert Briffault *(The Making of Humanity);* and, especially, John Elof Boodin *(A Realistic Universe, Cosmic Evolution* and *The Social Mind),* whose maxim—"the laws of thought are the laws of things"—appears at least twice in Steinbeck's work. There is documentary evidence that Steinbeck and Ricketts were familiar with all of these philosophers. From these central figures the circle of influence widens to the more conventional figures of Western and Eastern philosophy.

The influence of Jung's psychology is everywhere present. Although both collaborators shared holistic and organismal views of life and the universe (that every part is related to every other as in one super organism), they were sometimes divided in their thinking about society and its problems. It can be said, generally, that the laissez-faire tendency of the nonteleological thinking essay (chapter 14) and some other passages in the book are more Ricketts than Steinbeck. It was he who tended to oppose primitivism to "the virus of civilization." Thus *Sea of Cortez* does not indicate a change in Steinbeck's attitude from the active, engaged role which Steinbeck had played in the 1930's. In fact, upon returning from the Gulf of California, and before completing his work on the narrative, he went to Mexico to write and work upon a documentary film *(The Forgotten Village)*, encouraging backward Indian villages to accept medical aid.

Significantly, Ricketts, who visited Steinbeck on location, disagreed with his friend's notions of progress and went so far as to write his own script which he said was "motivated oppositely" to that of Steinbeck. Although Steinbeck had written *Tortilla Flat* in praise of indolence, and was soon to write *Cannery Row,* rejecting the Western values of materialism and activism, these are both, in a sense, escapist novels. They are fictive versions of the free speculation which he liked to carry on with Ed Ricketts.

Concerning the relationship of *Sea of Cortez* to Steinbeck's other works, it can be said that there is hardly an idea in the novels preceding *East of Eden* which is not found in this journal. Compare the relationship of group-man concepts as elucidated in *In Dubious Battle* and *The Grapes of Wrath* to the observation on the characteristics of school fish in *Sea of Cortez;* the description of La Paz as a "colonial animal" in *The Pearl* and the social dynamics of Monterey in *Tortilla Flat* and *Cannery Row* to the colonial pelagic tunicates in *Sea of Cortez;* the Jungian race memory in *To a God Unknown* and *The Winter of Our Discontent* to the passage on the vestigial gill slits of the human foetus in *Sea of Cortez;* the holistic and organismic views of life in *To a God Unknown* and *The Grapes of Wrath* to the passage on the merging of species in *Sea of Cortez;* the adaptations to a changing environment of the migrants in *The Grapes of Wrath* and the adaptations of species to a changing ecology in *Sea of Cortez.* Even, within limits, compare the doctrine of nonteleological thinking to certain aspects of *In Dubious Battle* and *The Grapes of Wrath* which seem to accept the social situation as part of a vastly complex "field" of forces making the assignment of blame or specific cause rather pointless. The relationship of "good," "bad," and survival values is discussed not only in *Cannery Row,* but in *Sea of Cortez* also. The theory of leadership in *In Dubious Battle* and *The Grapes of Wrath* receives its authority from biological observations in *Sea of Cortez.* Even Steinbeck's life-long suspicion and finally hatred of Communism finds its biological analogues in the "overornamentation" of species preceding their extinction, and the necessary elimination of the unusually swift and strong and intelligent, as well as the slow and weak, in schools of fish or herds of animals or flocks of birds.

But although *Sea of Cortez* can be read with great profit for understanding the relationship between Ricketts and Steinbeck and a fuller knowledge of the intellectual backgrounds of Steinbeck's fiction, it is above all a very entertaining book, full of gusto for all forms of life, and reverence for the known and unknowable universe.

Within two days of the publication of *Sea of Cortez*, the Japanese bombed Pearl Harbor, and the United States was plunged into the conflict that had been raging in Europe and which Steinbeck in that book had seen regretfully as further proof that war is "a diagnostic trait of Homo sapiens." His desire to help in the war effort resulted in *Bombs Away: The Story of a Bomber Team* (1942), a frankly propagandistic work whose text and photographs were calculated "to tell the whole people of the kind and quality of our Air Force, of the caliber of its men and of the excellence of its equipment." Nevertheless the writing was the result of extensive observation at various training bases and, while factual and expository, kept some of the qualities which had made the inter-chapters of *The Grapes of Wrath* so effective. It was suggested that Steinbeck conclude the book with a climactic bombing raid, but he refused on the grounds that since he had never experienced such a raid the writing might be false. Instead, the book ends very effectively with a squadron of bombers taking off on a mission: "And the deep growl of the engines shook the air, shook the world, shook the future."

His final contribution to the war effort was as a foreign correspondent for the New York *Herald Tribune*. His dispatches begin "Somewhere in England," dated June 20, 1943, and these continue into December of that year. These pieces were not published as a collection until 1958, under the title *Once There Was a War*. In his introduction to this volume, Steinbeck writes that reading them after so many years he realized that they were "period pieces, the attitudes archaic, the impulses romantic, and, in the light of everything that has happened since, perhaps the whole body of work untrue and warped and one-sided." And so they are. But the interesting question is to what extent these qualities are the inevitable result of imposed censorship and the necessity to provide propaganda to bolster public morale, and to what extent they are early signals of a lapse in Steinbeck's powers as a writer. Perhaps the two are not unrelated and, as Hemingway believed, the self-damage of writing at less than one's best is permanent.

Leaving military analysis and commentary to those presumably better qualified, Steinbeck addressed himself in these pieces to the "human interest" aspect of what he was observing in England, North Africa, and the invasion of Italy. The early dispatches continue the kind of accurate yet meaningfully organized observation of his California migrant-labor pieces, and the prose style carries an authority and dignity:

The troops in their thousands sit on their equipment on the dock. It is evening, and the first of the dimout lights come on. The men wear their helmets, which make them all look alike, make them look like long rows of mushrooms. . . . There are several ways of wearing a hat or cap. A man may express himself in the pitch or tilt of his hat, but not with a helmet. There is only one way to wear a helmet. It won't go on any other way. It sits level on the head, low over the eyes and ears, low on the back of the neck. With your helmet on you are a mushroom in a bed of mushrooms.

Scattered throughout the dispatches are other passages recalling Steinbeck's interest in group man, the social organism, and, in particular, Jungian psychology as observed in men who, under great stress and exhaustion, revert to unconscious or dreamlike and atavistic behavior.

Increasingly, however, this kind of observation gives way to the anecdote, the character sketch, and the colorful incident. Things as they were become displaced by the stock characters and jokes of any war. There is Private Big Train Mulligan the "operator"; there is the big crap game; the war souvenir, the lucky charm, etc. Of course the prose style adjusts to the new subject matter. The dispatches become more and more amusing and the incidents improbable. There is, for example, the account of how the leader of a commando unit correctly estimated the unusually long time—an hour—it would take them to make a night landing on an island off Naples containing "a very large torpedo works," cut the wires to the mainland, kill the German guards, and evacuate the Italian admiral and his wife who were being held hostage. You see, he knew it would take the admiral's wife a long time to pack! In fact, they had to make an extra trip in their little rubber boat just to get her trunk. Another account of how five Americans got eighty-seven well-armed Germans to surrender is written as a short story and spread over four dispatches. The basic incident may have been true, but Steinbeck's increasing attraction to this kind of material with appeal to a popular audience seriously undermines the more permanent value of these dispatches.

His next piece of reporting, after the war, was *A Russian Journal* (1948), for which his traveling companion, Robert Capa, provided the photographs. Although avoiding political observation and comment, and written in Steinbeck's flattest reportorial style, the book was of some interest for establishing the normality and humanity of a people whose country we were so nervously watching for signs of aggression. Steinbeck accomplishes this largely through intimate views of particular individuals and families, especially of the "lively and friendly" Georgian and Ukrainian farmers who although collectivized into "battalions" managed to retain their independent nature through small family plots, much like those he himself had advocated for the migrant workers of California. But although the book was an obvious gesture of good will toward Russia, Steinbeck nevertheless noted the stifling effect of censorship upon the arts and the depressing effects on everyone of regimentation and bureaucracy, which tended to discourage the unique individual for no perceivable advantage—not even the mediocre efficiency which in *Sea of Cortez* he had suspected to be the result of the "elimination of the swift, the clever, and the intelligent." In neither its content nor style, however, does *A Russian Journal* add to Steinbeck's stature as a keen observer of the world around him.

Beginning with his war dispatches in 1943, Steinbeck devoted an increasing amount of his energies to journalism. Although the 1950's saw the publication of four novels, he also published in this period at least seventy articles, essays, introductions, reviews, etc., including the biographical sketch "About Ed Ricketts" for *The Log From the Sea of Cortez*, the introduction to *Once There Was a War*, and an essay on his short novels. Much of this writing is in the form of travel articles on England, Ireland, Italy and France for *Holiday*, *Saturday Review*, *Punch*, and other periodicals. The articles on France (eighteen of them) were translated into French and published as *Un Americain à New York et à Paris*, although it is difficult to see why. The content of most of these travel essays is superficial and the manner puerile: "Vegetable War," a criticism of the way the British cook Brussels sprouts; "How to Fish in French," an observation on how to catch nothing; "Yank in Europe," a defense of American manners abroad. One cannot help feeling that the only motivation for these articles is the need to pay travel expenses. Another group of essays finds justification only in the popular reputation of their author: "Mail I've Seen," "Making of a New Yorker," "Always

Something to Do in Salinas," "My War with the Ospreys,"
etc. There are also frivolous pieces such as "Random Thoughts
on Random Dogs," about the tendency of dogs to resemble
their masters, and "More About Aristocracy," on the advan-
tages of establishing an American titled nobility. Several pieces
are popular nostalgia, such as "Jalopies I Cursed and Loved,"
"I Remember the Thirties," "A Primer of the Thirties," etc.
Steinbeck also found time to write three pieces attacking his
critics and reviewers.

Perhaps the only interesting, though slight, articles of the
period are four or five short essays on the American political
scene. Two of them, "How to Tell Good Guys from Bad Guys"
and "The Death of a Racket" provided some humor in the
downfall of Senator Joseph McCarthy and his persecution of
liberal American intellectuals through his technique of guilt by
association. Another article, "Madison Avenue and the Election," concerns national elections and the marketing of the
presidency. Steinbeck's own involvement in the elections of
1952 and 1956 was the result of his great admiration for Adlai
Stevenson, about whom he published a laudatory essay, "The
Stevenson Spirit"; a foreword to *Speeches of Adlai Stevenson;*
an open letter; and an exchange of letters called "Our Rigged
Morality." Novelist and statesman shared a deep concern for
the "creeping immorality" and "public hypocrisy" of their
time. There can be no doubt that Steinbeck's intense personal
admiration and the shock of Stevenson's second defeat in the
presidential election of 1956 did much to confirm Steinbeck in

the mood out of which came his next work of fiction, *The Winter of Our Discontent* (1961).

In the remaining seven years of his life Steinbeck published no fiction but devoted most of his time to articles, his "Letters to Alicia," and two books—*Travels with Charley* and *America and Americans*. Generally the articles follow the same undistinguished pattern of his publications in the fifties. In November 1965, he began his first series of articles in *Newsday*, a Long Island newspaper, which appeared more or less weekly for six months. These "Letters to Alicia" were addressed to Alice Patterson Guggenheim, who had edited the newspaper from its founding in 1940 to her death in 1963, and whom Steinbeck admired as a "great newspaper woman." At the beginning, these letters, intimate in tone and rather awkwardly addressed to a dead person, take up a wide variety of topics: the proper relationship of the artist to the political state (always a watchdog, never a servant); violence on TV (induces real violence); computer analysis of disease; his own efforts to stop smoking.

In late December, with the Steinbecks' arrival in Europe, these letters become for the most part accounts of their travels in England, Ireland, and Israel. With the exception of two letters dealing with his interest in Malory and, along with Dr. Vinaver, their searching for and finding of an Arthurian manuscript, these accounts of local gentry, customs, and legends are second-rate observations on unimportant topics. The letters from Israel mark a great change in tone. In that country Steinbeck found much to admire in the people's great tenacity and capacity for work in face of the constant threat of extinction. These letters have an energy, a sense of purpose, and a preciseness of observation much in contrast to the whimsical looseness and chit-chat of his earlier correspondence in the series. Of particular interest to Steinbeck was the patriotic Israeli youth, whom he contrasted pointedly with the degenerate, lazy youth of the United States and the Western countries.

On the home scene, he respected the good intentions of some of the marchers on Washington who were protesting the Vietnam war, but he believed them naive and deluded. He saw our presence in Vietnam as a political necessity, a block to the Chinese, and actually compared the protesters to those who had attended the Nazi bund rallies in Madison Square Garden before Pearl Harbor and to the Tories of the American Revolution. The prisoners released by the North Vietnamese, who spoke against the war, he thought had been tortured or brainwashed. He suspected the draft-card burners and most draft-deferred college students of being motivated by the desire to avoid serving their country.

This attack upon youth together with his support of the Vietnam war make up, almost exclusively, the short remainder of his writing career and account for the alienation that Steinbeck suffered from the liberal element of American society, and for his declining reputation abroad. In December 1966 Steinbeck began his second series of "Letters to Alicia" announcing that he would soon be traveling to Asia to see the situation for himself. He wished that the Russian poet Yevtushenko, with whom he had exchanged opinions on Vietnam, could travel with him to both South and North Vietnam to discover the truth together. Later, on the scene, he invited other American writers—naming Arthur Miller, Saul Bellow, John Updike, Tennessee Williams—actually to come to *see* what they had such strong opinions about, reminding them of their duty as writers to know their subject.

For about two months Steinbeck observed the war in Vietnam at close hand. He went on bombing and strafing missions, dangerous, low-flying visual reconnaissance flights and patrols both by land and riverboat. He was dropped by helicopter in advance positions, visited the Demilitarized Zone and most major cities and important provinces of South Vietnam. On one of his expeditions he was accompanied by General Westmoreland himself. He learned how to fire the new weapons, so as not to be a deadweight in an emergency, and once actually pulled the lanyard of a large artillery piece. Steinbeck spared no danger to himself in order to see as much as he could of the conflict. Leaving Vietnam, he traveled for three more months in Thailand, Laos, Indonesia, and Bali; he wanted to visit North Vietnam and China, but was refused permission.

As might be expected, Steinbeck's firsthand observations only strengthened his earlier views. He expressed admiration for the American military personnel as opposed to the youth at home, whose energies would be far better spent helping the South Vietnamese rebuild their villages rather than carrying placards and protesting everything. Aware of his growing reputation as a "hawk" and a warmonger, he described some Vietcong atrocities and wished his critics could see them. He accused American newspapers of refusing to print such things, and he was scornful of "the screams of outrage against us when we do something by accident which the communists do regularly, coldly and by plan."

Despite these statements, however, it cannot be assumed that Steinbeck was a dupe or the tool of capitalist imperialism. He saw clearly, and described, the corrupt politics, economic exploitation, and suppression of the individual under the American-supported government in South Vietnam and under Sukarno in Indonesia. But he felt that outside of our own intervention the only alternative was occupation by the Chinese Communists, and that would be worse. The short-term gains of Communism for the common people would be paid for at the enduring expense of the free individual, the most valuable thing there is. Furthermore, his hatred of Communism did not blind him to the necessity of living with it as peacefully as possible. He strongly advised trade with Red China—even at a temporary loss to our own economy—as a far better tool of influence than war. In the remaining year of his life, Steinbeck was to become somewhat disillusioned with our stalemate presence in Southeast Asia and modified these views. But the widely syndicated "Letters to Alicia" had done their job, and it is on them that public opinion about Steinbeck's last phase presently rests.

The only work of more than passing interest in Steinbeck's

last phase is *Travels with Charley: In Search of America* (1962). Upon his return from England late in 1959, Steinbeck realized that for some time now he had been observing the changes in his own country "only from books and newspapers," that he had "not felt the country for twenty years," and hence "was writing of something I did not know about." So, shortly after Labor Day 1960, he set out to see the country by way of a pick-up truck specially equipped for comfortable camping. This he named *Rocinante,* and accompanied by a Sancho Panza in the form of Charley, his poodle, set forth not unlike Don Quixote himself. He returned home before Christmas, having been in thirty-four states and having covered ten thousand miles in a counterclockwise circle which took him from Long Island to Maine, across the northern states and down the coast to his familiar California scenes, returning across the southern states.

Ironically, there is very little in the 245 pages of *Travels with Charley* that Steinbeck could not have written without ever leaving New York. For he had not really lost touch with his country, but had purposefully insulated himself from a reality with which he felt increasingly uncomfortable, in which he could no longer immerse himself. Yet he could not altogether turn his back, either. He was motivated by a Whitmanesque compulsion to identify with and speak for the whole country. That this compulsion would be frustrated is suggested in the very first incident of his journey, the encounter with a submarine crewman anxious for duty on an atomic vessel, confident he would get used to staying under for three months at a time. "It's his world, not mine anymore," thinks Steinbeck. "It's his world now. Perhaps he understands things I will never learn." Only a quarter along the way, he is overcome with doubts about the value of his effort: "I came with the wish to learn what America is like. And I wasn't sure I was learning anything. I found I was talking aloud to Charley." It is this sense of alienation that persists throughout his comments upon the people and scenes he visited, persists in spite of occasional strident attempts to celebrate "the other things I know are there" but of which he can gather only scattered intimations. By the time he reaches the halfway point he has already lost even the illusion of "discovering America." He notes that his "impressionable gelatin plate was getting muddled" and determines "to inspect two more sections and call it a day—Texas and a sampling of the Deep South." Ten pages later he admits what he has "concealed" from himself—that he has been driving himself, pounding out the miles because he is "no longer hearing or seeing," that he has passed his "limit of taking in," that he is "helpless to assimilate anymore." The returning half of his trip is covered in just sixty pages. At the end of the book, he admits again that his journey was over before he returned home.

Perhaps it was over even before he left, for in addition to his alienation he took with him all the baggage of the third-rate journalist who sees only the stereotype and the cliché. We are never presented with the way it really was, but rather with manipulated "set-ups," experiences and conversations upon which he can lecture Charley or us about one of his two favorite topics—how Americans are all different and yet unique and homogeneous, or how everything seems to be going to hell but it isn't really.

Travels with Charley should have had as its subtitle not "In Search of America," but, after Thomas Wolfe, "You Can't Go Home Again." Steinbeck's real search—like that of Don Quixote—is not for present reality but for an idealized past. This search approaches its climax in Johnny Garcia's bar in Monterey, Steinbeck's old home ground. He not only resists Johnny's plea that nothing essential has changed, actually quoting the title of Wolfe's novel, but also insists that with the past "the greatest part of what we were is dead," and the new reality "perhaps good" is "nothing we can know." Speaking of Ed Ricketts, Joe Portagee, Flora Wood, and others now dead, Steinbeck insists that it is not these dear companions who are the true ghosts: "We're the ghosts." In the next scene, the climax of his search for America, Steinbeck goes to Fremont's Peak, a spot familiar to his youth and from which he can survey the entire world of his childhood, his "Long Valley": "I printed it once more on my eyes, south, west, and north, and then we hurried away from the permanent and changeless past. . . ." Just sixty pages later, he is back in New York, having discovered what he already knew, that he was caught between two Americas, one dead and the other a stranger.

It is doubtful that his next book four years later, *America and*

Americans, was a serious effort to improve that position, and more likely that it was a smart publishing venture following the great popular success of *Travels With Charley* and aimed at the same popular audience. The scant eighty-seven pages of text and many photographs contain nothing new, being frequently a verbatim repetition of observations about America ransacked from his previous work—*The Winter of Our Discontent,* the "Letters to Alicia," letters to Adlai Stevenson, *The Short Reign of Pippin IV,* even *The Grapes of Wrath*—but especially *Travels with Charley.* Even more than in the latter work, Steinbeck speaks from a position of stasis not only between past and present ("the roads of the past have come to an end and we have not yet discovered a path to the future. I think we will find one, but its direction may be unthinkable to us now"), but between the polar qualities of both Americans and America. As Steinbeck presents these qualities, they do not seem to exist in a dynamic pattern, a viable paradox, but simply to cancel each other out, leaving nothing. Clearly, despite all the whistling, Steinbeck is in the dark; *America and Americans* is the most depressing book he ever wrote, the more depressing because its author reveals but cannot admit his own profound despair. The true optimism that permitted man occasionally to "slip back, but only half a step" in *The Grapes of Wrath* gives way to the hysterical insistence that "we have never slipped back—never."

Eight years after Steinbeck's death, appeared *The Acts of King Arthur and his Noble Knights* (1976), his version of the

Morte d'Arthur, which had so fascinated him since childhood, and upon which he had been working for twelve years. But he had finished only a small fragment of the projected whole; and although his letters reveal he was as steeped in his material as many scholars of the period, they also reveal a vacillation and insecurity about style which is reminiscent of his struggles with *East of Eden.*

Although Steinbeck produced a respectable amount of nonfiction in his career, only *Sea of Cortez* (written in collaboration with Ricketts), his early pieces on migrant labor, and perhaps a few of his first dispatches as a war correspondent are of the quality one would expect from a writer of his unquestioned stature.

His real accomplishments are his eighteen volumes of fiction, and upon these his reputation rests secure. Among contemporary American novelists only William Faulkner approaches Steinbeck's variety of form and prose style. The range of Steinbeck's themes and subject matter is similarly impressive. Furthermore, he was able to achieve these things without losing the common touch. His ability to bring together in his novels and in his image of man both the scientifically described world and that of the intuition and imagination, nature and myth, without distorting either, that is Steinbeck's own unique genius.

A SELECTED BIBLIOGRAPHY

By Steinbeck

FICTION
1929   *Cup of Gold*
1932   *The Pastures of Heaven*
1933   *To a God Unknown*
1935   *Tortilla Flat*
1936   *In Dubious Battle*
1937   *Of Mice and Men*
       The Red Pony
1938   *The Long Valley*
1939   *The Grapes of Wrath*
1941   *The Forgotten Village* (film story and photographs)
1942   *The Moon Is Down*
1945   *Cannery Row*
1947   *The Pearl*
       The Wayward Bus
1950   *Burning Bright*
1952   *East of Eden*
1954   *Sweet Thursday*
1957   *The Short Reign of Pippin IV*
1961   *The Winter of Our Discontent*
1975   *Viva Zapata!* (screenplay) edited by Robert Morsberger

NONFICTION
1938   *Their Blood Is Strong* (pamphlet)
1941   *Sea of Cortez* (with Edward F. Ricketts)
1942   *Bombs Away: The Story of a Bomber Team*
1948   *A Russian Journal*
1951   *The Log from the Sea of Cortez* (containing "About Ed Ricketts")
1958   *Once There Was a War*
1962   *Travels with Charley: In Search of America*
1966   *America and Americans*

POSTHUMOUS WORKS
1969   *Journal of a Novel*
1975   *Steinbeck: A Life in Letters,* edited by Elaine Steinbeck and Robert Wallsten
1976   *The Acts of King Arthur and His Noble Knights*

About Steinbeck

Astro, Richard. *John Steinbeck and Edward F. Ricketts: The Shaping of a Novelist.* Minneapolis: University of Minnesota Press, 1973.

————, and Hayashi, Tetsumaro, eds. *Steinbeck: The Man and His Work.* Corvallis: Oregon State University Press, 1971.

Davis, Robert Murray, ed. *Steinbeck: A Collection of Critical Essays.* Englewood Cliffs, New Jersey: Prentice-Hall, 1972.

Donohue, Agnes McNeill, ed. *A Casebook on "The Grapes of Wrath."* New York: Thomas Y. Crowell, 1968.

Fontenrose, Joseph Eddy. *John Steinbeck: An Introduction and Interpretation.* New York: Barnes and Noble, 1963 (Holt, Rinehart and Winston, Paperback edition).

French, Warren, ed. *A Companion to "The Grapes of Wrath."* New York: Viking Press, 1963 (contains "The Harvest Gypsies").

_____. *John Steinbeck.* Boston: Twayne, 1975.

Hayashi, Tetsumaro. *A New Steinbeck Bibliography (1929–1971).* Metuchen, New Jersey: Scarecrow Press, 1973.

_____, ed. *Steinbeck's Literary Dimension: A Guide to Comparative Studies.* Metuchen, New Jersey: Scarecrow Press, 1973.

_____, ed. *A Study Guide to Steinbeck's "The Long Valley."* Ann Arbor, Michigan: Pierian Press, 1974.

Levant, Howard. *The Novels of John Steinbeck: A Critical Study.* Columbia: University of Missouri Press, 1974.

Lisca, Peter, ed. *John Steinbeck, "The Grapes of Wrath": Text and Criticism.* New York: Viking Press, 1972.

_____. *The Wide World of John Steinbeck.* New Brunswick, New Jersey: Rutgers University Press, 1958.

Marks, Lester J. *Thematic Continuity in the Novels of John Steinbeck.* The Hague, The Netherlands: Mouton, 1969 (New York: Humanities Press, 1969).

Modern Fiction Studies (Spring, 1965). A special number devoted to Steinbeck, with a checklist of criticism devoted to his work.

Moore, Harry Thornton. *The Novels of John Steinbeck: A First Critical Study.* Chicago: Normandie House, 1939; Port Washington, New York: Kennikat, 1968.

Tedlock, Ernest W., Jr. and Wicker, C. V., eds. *Steinbeck and His Critics: A Record of Twenty-Five Years.* Albuquerque: University of New Mexico Press, 1957.

Watt, Frank W. *John Steinbeck.* London: Oliver and Boyd, 1962; New York: Grove Press, 1962.

Index